Published by Christian Art Publishers
PO Box 1599, Vereeniging, 1930, RSA

© 2017
First edition 2017

Designed by Christian Art Publishers

Images used under license from Shutterstock.com

Scripture quotations are taken from the *Holy Bible*, New International Version® NIV®.
Copyright © 1973, 1978, 1984 by International Bible Society.
Used by permission of Zondervan Publishing House.
All rights reserved.

Scripture quotations are taken from the *Holy Bible*, English Standard Version.
Copyright © 2001 by Crossway Bibles, a division of Good News Publishers.
Used by permission. All rights reserved.

Printed in China

ISBN 978-1-64272-637-4

© All rights reserved. No part of this book may be reproduced in any form
without permission in writing from the publisher, except in the case of
brief quotations in critical articles or reviews.

In Christ Alone

Victor Kuligin
&
Robert Yarbrough

CONTENTS

1. Sol...
2. Sol...
3. Sol...
4. Solu...
5. Sol...

Preface — page 7

Scriptura
by Scripture Alone — page 23

Gratia
by Grace Alone — page 43

Fide
through Faith Alone — page 63

Christus
in Christ Alone — page 83

Deo Gloria
for the Glory of God Alone — page 103

A Final Word — page 123

End Notes — page 128

Dedication

In 1900, African Protestants were 1.7% of the world Protestant population. By 2000 it was 33.5%. The projection for mid-2017 is 40.8%. By 2050, 53.1% of Protestants in the world will be in Africa. This does not count African Protestants on other continents.[1]

This book is dedicated to the memory of all African Christian martyrs, but especially those who made the good confession as Protestants.

> I charge you in the presence of God, who gives life to all things, and of Christ Jesus, who in his testimony before Pontius Pilate made the good confession.

1 Timothy 6:13

Preface

"In Christ Alone."

A song by that title is sung in congregations around the world. The first verse celebrates the riches He offers:

> In Christ alone my hope is found,
> He is my light, my strength, my song;
> This Cornerstone, this solid Ground,
> Firm through the fiercest drought and storm.
> What heights of love, what depths of peace,
> When fears are stilled, when strivings cease!
> My Comforter, my All in All,
> Here in the love of Christ I stand.[1]

"Christ alone": no one but he can provide what this song, dating from 2001, celebrates.

But the basis for the song is far older than 2001. This "Christ" who grants such hope, light, strength, and much else is Jesus, son of Mary, but also Son of God. Like the Son, God the Father too is "alone"—unmatched, unequaled, unparalleled, as Scriptures dating from 1000 B.C. testify:

Psalm 62:1

*For **God alone** my soul waits in silence;
from him comes my salvation.*

Psalm 62:5

*For **God alone**, O my soul, wait in silence,
for my hope is from him.*

Psalm 71:16

*With the mighty deeds of the Lord G<small>OD</small> I will come;
I will remind them of your righteousness, yours **alone**.*

Psalm 72:18

*Blessed be the L<small>ORD</small>, the **God** of Israel,
who **alone** does wondrous things.*

Psalm 86:10

*For you are great and do wondrous things;
you **alone** are **God**.*

Whether you are a contemporary songwriter or the ancient psalmist, Christ and the Father who sent him to redeem the world are unique—They "alone" stand behind the creation of the world, its daily sustenance, and its eventual redemption.

In fact, the very name of one Old Testament prophet celebrates the sublime singularity of God: "Micah" means "Who is like God?" It is a question tinged with awe. God answers: "I am God, and there is no other; I am God, and there is none like me" (Isa. 46:9).

This book celebrates the sole source of ultimate hope and meaning in this world and the next: Jesus Christ the Lord, the Son of the true and living God. "The Lord is the true God; he is the living God and the everlasting King" (Jer. 10:10).

Just One Way? Really?

Marketers say that in modern societies, twenty-first-century people want choices. Isn't "Christ alone" a limited selection? Aren't we denying endless possibilities if we push language of uniqueness too far when it comes to questions of religion, the divine, and human knowledge of such matters?

"Christ alone" isn't limiting if it is, in Jesus' words, the truth that sets us free (John 8:32).

The dedication of this book speaks of the meteoric growth of Christianity in Africa, and particularly Protestant Christianity with its focus on the Bible and its message of salvation in Jesus. Much of Africa is Muslim. Here is a Muslim's testimony to the vast difference he detected between his ancestral religion (Islam) and an approach to God that considers "Christ alone" (which of course Islam condemns).

This Muslim man named Amid found a Koran in his language (like many Muslims he cannot speak or read Arabic). He discovered that the Koran had no plan of salvation within it. "No titles of honor for Muhammad in the Koran, but 23 honorable titles that Allah gave to Isa [Jesus]. I saw that Muhammad is dead, but Isa is alive in heaven with Allah now. Muhammad is not coming again, but Isa will come again at the last judgment. Only four times does the Koran speak of Muhammad, and yet 97 times it talks about Isa. Muhammad is not a savior, but *Isa's* very name means 'savior.' Muhammad is only a messenger, but Isa is called *Ruhullah*, the Spirit of Allah."[2]

Many—even Muslims—are discovering new meaning and hope for their lives by taking a fresh look at the God who really cannot be compared to any other: "You shall have no other gods before me" (Exod. 20:3; Deut. 5:7). Christ (God the Son) underscored how he and he alone makes God real and present to us when he said, "I and the Father are one" (John 10:30). Or again, "Whoever has seen me has seen the Father" (John 14:9).

This mysterious pronouncement of Christ's unity with God the Father is affirmed in the statement: "No one has ever seen God; <u>the only God, who is at the Father's side,</u> he has made him known" (John 1:18). Note the underlined words. Those words refer to Christ. Christ alone.[3]

The Struggle to Give Christ His Due

From the earliest days of the church, Jesus' uniqueness was confessed.

Acts 4:12

There is salvation in no one else,
for there is no other name under heaven
given among men by which we must be saved.

1 Corinthians 8:6

For us there is one God, the Father,
from whom are all things and for whom we exist,
and one Lord, Jesus Christ, through whom
are all things and through whom we exist.

1 Timothy 2:5

For there is one God, and there is one mediator
between God and men, the man Christ Jesus.

Over the centuries, though, the church struggled to keep Christ and the gospel message at the center of its faith and practice. Some groups lapsed back into Jewish practices. Others adopted Hellenistic philosophies and concocted an aberrant form of Christianity later called Gnosticism.

After Christianity became recognized as the Roman Empire's religion (early 4th century), it was endangered by political entanglements and interventions. When reformers founded monasteries (for men) and nunneries (for women) during the Middle Ages, some thought that salvation lay in holy orders—it was only for those who left lay life and joined monastic religious communities. It wasn't "Christ alone" but "the radical commitment of my entire life and withdrawal from society" that might guarantee God's acceptance.

By the end of the Middle Ages (15-16th centuries), the Western (Roman Catholic) church had arrived at teachings and practices that were not always grounded in God's Word the Bible. This resulted in the church straying from a proper emphasis on "Christ alone" as the head of the church (on earth the pope was viewed as head).

The Reformation beginning about 1517 was an attempt to restore Christ and Scripture to their rightful place of supremacy: Christ to save his people and rule as Lord over all, Scripture as a set of unique writings given by God to point sinners to the saving message of salvation by grace through faith in Christ.

> The saving message: Salvation by grace through faith in Christ.

The Reformation's main emphases have been summed up in five statements using the word "alone" (Latin *sola*):

1. **Sola Scriptura** — *by Scripture Alone*
2. **Sola Gratia** — *by Grace Alone*
3. **Sola Fide** — *through Faith Alone*
4. **Solus Christus** — *in Christ Alone*
5. **Soli Deo Gloria** — *for the Glory of God Alone*

This book is an explanation and in places celebration of those solas. At the time of the Reformation and still today, they represent a serious, and often successful, attempt to place Christ back at the center of church proclamation, Christian practice, and individuals' approach to God.[4]

"Christ Alone" Today

Many feel that the Reformation largely succeeded in reaffirming Christ as the key to salvation rather than church tradition, ritual, or human piety. But since that time, just as throughout church history, Christians have struggled to maintain the goal "that in everything he might be preeminent" (Col. 1:18).

At present, there are many proposals or practices that effectively de-center Christ. In much academic theology, Jesus' divinity and the Bible's accuracy are denied.

A professor at Yale Divinity School in the United States declares, "A main goal of my writing is to take orthodoxy [Christian teaching as confessed through the centuries] out of the hands of conservative Christians and to show . . . how to read the Bible beyond historical criticism."[5]

A result of this professor's reading is to view the persons of the Trinity—Father, Son, and Holy Spirit—in "queer terms."[6] "The multiple genders of God" allow us "to make sacred the multiple genders people experience": "not only male and female but also transgendered, transsexual, intersexed and simultaneously multiple gendered roles or identities."[7]

This is a far cry from Christ's simple appeal to Genesis: "Have you not read that he who created them from the beginning made them male and female, and said, 'Therefore a man shall leave his father and his mother and hold fast to his wife, and the two shall become one flesh'?" (Matt. 19:4-5). The Yale professor has exchanged "Christ alone" for convictions and practices that neither Christ, the Christian Scriptures, nor societies through history worldwide have usually thought to be healthy or normal.

Some preaching of Christ gives the impression that the goal of religion in his name is to benefit his followers by pouring out wealth and prosperity—if only you have enough faith! Related to this are figures and movements that focus on healing or other miraculous events.

In this view, Christ's role is to empower people now to do the kinds of miracles they imagine they see in Scripture.

But what if those miracles were primarily signs to point to the truth of the message of Jesus' Lordship, and salvation through faith in him? Then the point of the Bible's miracles is to promote faith in Christ for all those who hear the gospel message. The miracles support our resolve to live as his disciples in the pursuit of making other disciples (Matt. 28:19-20), not on a regular basis to imitate Jesus and the apostles in the miracles they performed.

Others enthrone politics in the name of Christ. For some this means left-wing views and practices. Christ becomes the inspiration for Marxist initiatives, for example. For others this means right wing views, including nationalism, perhaps militarism, and certainly anger towards those who disagree.

Of course leftists are often angry too, even in the church. Both conservative and progressive political outlooks run the risk of taking God's name in vain by twisting "Christ alone" to support the outlook that "we alone" in our political party are on the side of the angels. M. Craig Barnes has written rightly of pastors: "We are not cheerleaders who lead the congregation in fight songs for our side of a political game."[8] It can be tempting, but that would be a betrayal of "Christ alone."

The Promise of "Christ Alone" Conviction

At the personal level, communion with God through forgiveness of sin and new life "in Christ alone" offers the prospects of the deepest imaginable inner health and contentment:

> Do not be anxious about anything, but in everything by prayer and supplication with thanksgiving let your requests be made known to God. And the peace of God, which surpasses all understanding, will guard your hearts and your minds in Christ Jesus. (Phil. 4:6-7)

These words, written by the apostle Paul during one of his several imprisonments, testifies to the stability and hope God offers through a life of faith in Christ and devotion to the mission to which he calls his followers.

At the international level, preaching and teaching pointing to "Christ alone" in the sense of the sole sufficiency of His cross and resurrection for our redemption has resulted in the most dramatic growth in Christianity ever witnessed. An African historian at Yale (with very different convictions from the Yale professor cited previously) puts it well: around the world, "new communities have embraced Christianity, with implications for a fresh understanding of the gospel in world history."[9]

This is seen, for example, in China. First Catholic and then Protestant missionaries labored there without much success prior to the mid-twentieth century. At that time the Communist government expelled all missionaries. It was estimated that only a half million or fewer Chinese Christians remained. They were persecuted mercilessly by the atheistic government.

Yet once on their own, and despite their suffering, Chinese Christians began to multiply. Rodney Stark and Xiuhua Wang have chronicled and documented the spread of Christian faith there. Here is a table from their book.[10] It assumes the rate of growth (7%) that can be documented over recent decades:

Year	Number of Christians in China (Catholic and Protestant) in millions
1980	10.0
1990	19.7
2000	38.7
2007	61.1
2010	76.1
2014	99.8
2020	149.7 (325 million is current United States population)
2030	294.6
2040	579.5

Within less than five years, there will be more Christians in China than in the United States. Sometime in the 2030s, the number of Christians will surpass the total number of United States citizens.

Results alone are not a test of truth. But the message of Christ in the Reformation spirit of "Christ alone" has resulted in personal conversions and church growth that are staggering to contemplate.

Another indicator of the promise of proclaiming Christ as the sole hope for our salvation is missionary outreach. Patrick Johnstone in *The Future of the Global Church* writes of "the expansion of the mission force in the 20th century."[11] He states:

> The mobilization of Christians in missions since 1900 has been astonishing. From 17,400 in 1900, the number rose slowly to 43,000 in 1962, but then came the explosive growth that followed the Awakening around that time, with some 200,000 [missionaries] in 2000 and maybe even 300,000 in 2010. This has happened even as non-evangelical denominational missions collapsed, with the new wave of fervent evangelical missionaries more than replacing them.

Currently the number of foreign missionaries—increasingly from countries like Brazil, South Korea, Nigeria, and China, not from the West—has been placed at 430,000. It is projected to rise to 700,000 by 2050.[12]

The word of "Christ alone" has done and will continue to do a world-changing work in multiplying the missionaries who go forth spreading that word whatever the cost.

The Price and Power of "Christ Alone" Conviction

Christ told his first followers: "In the world you will have tribulation. But take heart; I have overcome the world" (John 16:33). From the beginning, Christianity has had its martyrs. The tribulation of Christians presently should be making international headlines, though it is commonly downplayed if not ignored or suppressed.

Around the world in our times and for many years, Jesus' warning of tribulation has proven well-founded. One agency says 1,207 Christians a year die as martyrs.[13] That's about 3.3 a day. By another reckoning 90,000 die a year.[14] That's 247 a day. That number is projected to remain stable until around 2025, then rise to about 100,000 annually.[15]

What gives so many people courage to stand by their convictions when their very lives are threatened? It is surely the conviction that in Christ alone is salvation, supported no doubt by the very real sense that Christ is present with His people in their hour of direst need.

Yale church historian and Gambian native Lamin Sanneh was asked whether Western skepticism of Christianity discouraged him. His implied "no" took this form: "What sustains me is the sheer power of the story that is represented by the lives of the individual men and women whose faith and devotion reinforce the veracity of the apostolic witness."[16] Yes, there is tribulation. But as Jesus projected, his followers take heart, for he has overcome so they may endure in faith.

Who Else but Christ?

Long ago the prophet Jeremiah lamented, "The heart is deceitful above all things, and desperately sick; who can understand it?" (Jer. 17:9). Many would agree that worldwide, human affairs are in a mess, to say nothing of alarming environmental indicators. Is there anything or anyone who can make a difference? Many have concluded that it is folly to put ultimate hope in any one human, nation, movement, or philosophy. Peoples totter between fanaticism and despair.

When the need is great, the solution must be still greater.

A skier recently found himself in such need.[17] He fell into a "tree well" of loose and deep snow around the base of a tree. His companion attempted to rescue him. The trouble was that his companion was his nine-year-old son. The boy struggled valiantly to free his father but to no avail. Eventually the ski patrol succeeded in removing him. But the snow had been suffocating. Resuscitation efforts were unsuccessful.

This book aims at commending a solution to the human plight—personal and global—sufficient for successful rescue of all those who hear and heed. That plight is addressed abundantly and eternally "in Christ alone," as chapters to follow hope to affirm. In each chapter, the authors highlight a key Reformation church leader who was instrumental in espousing that particular "sola," with ample biblical proof supporting it. Lastly, practical implications of each "sola" are provided, showing that "in Christ alone" is as relevant today as it was 2000 years ago when Jesus proclaimed,

> "I am the way,
> and the truth,
> and the life.
> No one comes to the Father
> except through me."
>
> **JOHN 14:6**

1

Sola

> "When the divine quality of Scripture ... has been accepted, its infallibility follows of necessity."[1]
> **FRANCIS TURRETIN**

Scriptura
by Scripture Alone

Franz Turretini

1623-1687

(better known in English circles as Francis Turretin) was a Swiss-Italian theologian and churchman who strenuously argued for the inspiration and inerrancy of God's Word. Turretin taught Reformed doctrine in Geneva, continuing the legacy of John Calvin. For Turretin, the fundamental principle for all theology done rightly was that the Bible was the sole communication from God upon which correct pronouncements of faith and doctrine could be made. Turretin lived at the beginning of the Enlightenment, that "Age of Reason" in Western civilization that eventually eroded any respect for the Bible as the inspired, infallible Word of God.

By Scripture Alone

*All Scripture is breathed out by God
and profitable for teaching, for reproof,
for correction, and for training in righteousness,
that the man of God may be complete,
equipped for every good work.*
2 TIMOTHY 3:16-17

Five hundred years ago, the central debate in the Reformation protest against Medieval Roman Catholicism was the proper place of the Bible. Was it merely one of several avenues of God's revelation? Did it sit alongside the Church, which has equal authority to Scripture? Or was God's Word in some way unique, singular in its authority and sufficiency?

Answering these questions is not merely an academic exercise; these are life and death issues. What Scripture communicates is not the ephemeral realities of yesteryear, it is none other than God's authoritative mandate to fallen humanity about how to get right with him. Eternal issues are at stake; souls are won or lost depending upon the answers to these questions.

Thus, the Protestant Reformation was born out of a question of authority. What should a Christian do when the Church declares a doctrine that contradicts biblical teaching as dogma (i.e., a point of theology that all Christians must believe)? If the Pope creates another indulgence (an ecclesial pronouncement the purchasing of which grants time off from the temporary punishments of Purgatory), should a believer obtain one? Upon what authority do Christians base their opinions when it comes to godly issues of faith and piety?

The Character of God Is the Character of Scripture

The Protestant ethos rests in the knowledge that God is known through his Word, and that his Word is a reflection of his character. Because it is impossible for God to lie (Heb. 6:18), evangelicals have long asserted that God's Word also cannot lie. Its declarations are infallible and inerrant. This agrees with the Old Testament assertion that God's Word is "perfect," "sure," "right," "pure" and "true" (Ps. 19:7-9). It is why the psalmist can say that God's Word is a light and lamp for his life, and why he puts his hope in it (Ps. 119:105, 114).

As such, the Apostle Peter can claim that God's Word is "imperishable" (1 Pet. 1:23) and "remains forever" (1 Pet. 1:25), echoing the teaching of Jesus in the Sermon on the Mount (Matt. 5:18). This is also why in his priestly prayer, Jesus asks that the Father set apart his disciples from the world, highlighting Scripture's importance: "Sanctify them in the truth; your word is truth" (John 17:17).

Paul writes to his protégé Timothy that Scripture is inspired by God. The Greek word Paul uses is *theopneustos*, literally "God-breathed" (2 Tim. 3:16). Because it is breathed out by God, this Word can save you (James 1:21). The prophet Isaiah declares that God's Word does everything it is sent by God to do (Isa. 55:10-11), and the prophet Jeremiah likens it to a "hammer that breaks the rock in pieces" (Jer. 23:29).

God's Word is of such a character that Paul can speak of it metaphorically like this:

> For the word of God is living and active, sharper than any two-edged sword, piercing to the division of soul and of spirit, of joints and of marrow, and discerning the thoughts and intentions of the heart. (Heb. 4:12)

The ministry of God's Spirit and God's Word go hand-in-hand. It is the sword of the Spirit (Eph. 6:17), and Paul exhorts believers to "let the word of Christ dwell in you richly" (Col. 3:16).

This means that the Bible does not merely contain the words of God, but rather that every word of Scripture is God's word. To ignore or reject anything in the Bible is to ignore or reject God himself. Every truth claimed in Scripture calls for unqualified acceptance. If God commands us, we must obey. If he promises something, it surely will be fulfilled. If he warns us, we had better heed it.

> The Bible does not merely contain the words of God, but rather that every word of Scripture is God's word.

Unfortunately, many Christians have a rather cavalier view of Scripture. Its relevance is questioned; its authority ignored. The book tends to sit on the shelf during the week, perhaps dusted off and taken to church Sunday morning, if that. However, to say that the Bible is unimportant, or should be relegated to a side position in our faith, is like saying that oxygen isn't all that important for us to breathe, or that food and water should be given a minor role in sustaining our lives.

Jesus provides us with the proper perspective concerning God's holy Word when he quotes the Mosaic Law: "Man shall not live by bread alone, but by every word that comes from the mouth of God" (Matt. 4:4; Deut. 8:3).

When we sum up all the things the Bible has to say about God's Word, we see just how vital it is to the believer's life:

- We cannot understand the Gospel without the Word of God
- We cannot know Jesus without the Word of God
- We cannot become like Jesus without the Word of God
- We cannot be sanctified and purified without the Word of God
- We cannot be saved without the Word of God
- We cannot grow in holiness without the Word of God
- We cannot love our fellow believers without the Word of God
- We cannot be equipped for every good work without the Word of God
- We have no hope without the Word of God.

All this underlines the authority, necessity and sufficiency of God's inspired and inerrant Word for the Christian.

Whose Opinion Matters?

This means that when it comes to divine matters, all secondary sources of authority such as church tradition or ecclesiastical teaching or personal preference must be in submission to God's Word. This makes good sense. If someone were to ask me, "What is Paris like in the summer?" my opinion would only be as good as the opinion of someone who has actually been there and experienced the city (I have not). When it comes to godly matters, a person's opinion is only valid if it agrees with God's opinion.

We must immediately dispel the post-modern myth that our opinion is intrinsically valuable. It is not if it is wrong. Any opinion concerning godly things – who God is, how we can have a relationship with him, the features of the afterlife – must correspond to someone who has authority on these matters. That someone, of course, is God.

> When it comes to godly matters, a person's opinion is only valid if it agrees with God's opinion.

Consider answering the following questions: What happened at the creation of the universe? If God is holy and I am a sinner, how am I going to get right with him? What does the "throne room" of heaven look like? It should become immediately obvious that the lone person qualified to answer these inquiries is God. He alone sits in a position to grant infallible answers to these queries because he is the only one who possesses perfect perspective on reality.

I am consistently dumbfounded by people – many of them Christians no less – who say things like, "God would never do such and such," when the Bible has him doing exactly that. "God accepts everyone who is sincere in their beliefs." "God would never eternally judge people who have not heard the Gospel and had a chance to choose." "God loves everybody equally; we are all his children." Such platitudes are only as good as the authority upon which they are based.

Unfortunately, though, people who say such things often have little support for their views. Their opinion rests on their opinion. They believe what they believe because they believe it. Their authority is nothing more than themselves.

"There is no rainfall in Paris in the summer." Someone who knows Paris immediately knows how preposterous that statement is. Unfortunately, many people make equally absurd statements about God, his nature, and his plans for humanity, simply because they do not know God's Word.

Consider how foolhardy it is to declare truths about God that God has not declared about himself. In fact, we can never say something true about God unless God has first revealed that fact about himself. Our pronouncements about God are only as good as God's pronouncements about God. If you want to know who God is, ask God. Anything else is mindless speculation.

Imagine the foolishness of making a pronouncement about the afterlife when you have no firsthand knowledge of it. If you want to know what heaven or hell is like, consult Scripture. Supposed modern revelations about these places, especially embodied in people who claim to have "been there and back," are of no consequence. We already have the authoritative words of Jesus on this issue. Why would we need to consult somebody else?

If you want to know how to have a relationship with God – what we often call "salvation" – ask God about the matter. God is holy and eternal; humans are fallen and finite. How to be reconciled with the omnipotent Creator is not left to us to figure out. We cannot. Thankfully, God has laid out a way through his Son Jesus.

Speaking of which, our fallenness is not an accidental byproduct of some random event. It has come precisely because we have willingly rebelled against our Maker. To then expect these same fallen creatures to somehow discern the right way to God is sheer folly. Fortunately, Jesus has told us the right way, and it is only through him (John 14:6).

It is this truth that prompted John Calvin (1509-1564) to write, "For errors can never be uprooted from human hearts until true knowledge of God is planted therein."[2] That true knowledge comes solely from God's Word.

Perhaps now you begin to get a sense for why Protestants were willing to risk their lives for *sola Scriptura*. These issues bear eternal consequences. Get your relationship with God wrong and nothing else will matter. This means that you must have an authority that rightly explicates God's character and his plans for us. As Jesus and the apostles tell us, that authority is God's Word.

For this reason Martin Luther (1483-1546) could boldly proclaim, "a simple layman armed with Scripture is greater than the mightiest pope without it."[3]

> "A simple layman armed with Scripture is greater than the mightiest pope without it."
>
> **MARTIN LUTHER**

Practical Implications of *Sola Scriptura*

What can today's average Christian take away from the Protestant Reformation that occurred five centuries ago? I would like to highlight four practical repercussions of the Reformation ideal *sola Scriptura*.

1 Scripture is not one of many equal avenues of divine revelation from God.

This was the particular problem the Protestants addressed, specifically as it related to the authority of the Pope and the Magisterium, or teaching office, of the Roman Catholic Church. Medieval Roman Catholicism placed church tradition alongside the Bible as an equal stream of authority, with the ability to create doctrine not previously espoused by Scripture or the church. As such, doctrines like Purgatory, the immaculate conception and ascension of Mary, and the infallibility of the Pope all were created by the Magisterium, but have virtually no biblical support. Catholicism continues this trend today.

Casting our net wider, it is becoming popular, even in evangelical circles, to speak of other means of God's revelation that are on par with the Bible. For example, some Christians imply that God's general revelation through creation is adequate to be saved. However, as Paul clearly explains, all that sinners do with general revelation is warp and reject it (Rom. 1:18-23). The special revelation of God's Word is needed for sinners to rightly interpret God's general revelation.

Even further, some evangelicals have become open to other religions as means of God's saving revelation. It is not uncommon to hear Christians say that the God of Islam and the God of Christianity are the same, or to put the Quran on equal footing with the Bible. Let me be clear: Islam rejects the Trinity, the incarnation, the Bible as inerrant revelation from God, the personhood of the Spirit, and the deity, crucifixion, resurrection, and atonement of Jesus Christ. After all that, to declare the teaching of Mohammed as equal to that of Christ is nothing short of blasphemous.

If you want to know who the one true God is, and how to live a life pleasing to him, the Bible is the sole source for this divine revelation. As such, not only can it be trusted, but it must be.

2 Scripture is not simply the primary revelation from God.

Related to the issue above is the notion that God speaks in various other ways to Christians, such as through dreams or personal revelations, and that these experiences can be equally divine revelations from God, telling us what to believe and how to live. Scripture then becomes merely the *primary* way for God to reveal himself to the believer, not the only way.

Indeed, God is not limited in how he can communicate to us. However, this view tends to smuggle in the belief that these other forms of revelation are equally authoritative to Scripture and should be regularly expected in the believer's experience. It also has the tendency of eventually downplaying Scripture. After all, why rely on a 2000-year-old book when God's Spirit speaks to me directly?

3 Scripture is the only source for divine revelation, not all information.

Keep in mind, we are speaking about godly matters. *Sola Scriptura* does not apply, say, to how to make an omelet, or how far the earth is from the sun. However, in matters concerning divine revelation, the Bible must be our sole authority.

4 Secondary sources of authority are only good if they agree with Scripture.

Unfortunately, *sola Scriptura* has been abused by some Christians who feel that it gives them the right to proclaim truth from Scripture based on little more than their own personal interpretation. Certainly, God has given his Word to every one of his children, but proper understanding of that Word comes corporately as the Body of Christ, in exercising all the gifts of the Spirit, interprets and illumines truths from the Bible.

This is why the fathers of the Reformation never intended for private interpretations of Scripture to usurp the interpretation produced corporately by the church. Rather, the Reformers wanted the church to get back to the original interpretation of God's Word held by the apostles and early church fathers. Their desire was to *re-form* the church, not create a new one. They still recognized secondary sources of authority such as church councils and traditions.

In the abovementioned four ways, the Bible stands as the sole source of divine revelation for the Christian today. Ecclesiastical authorities are subject to correction by Scripture, as are individual interpretations.

Sola Scriptura rejects any claim for an original, infallible authority of divine revelation other than the Bible. In this sense, then, all other supposed "holy books" must be rejected by Christians, as must any mystical experience or teaching of the church that runs contrary to Scripture. All church traditions, creeds, confessions, councils, and teachings must conform to Scripture.

This has grander implications than simply individual salvation. Any Christian enterprise that does not stay true to God's Word is in danger of losing its eternal significance. Insofar as the Church remains true to Scripture can it be "salt and light" in the world. Only then can it expect God's favor.

This is why we must resist the constant tug away from God's Word that exists in worldly endeavors and even churches today that look to remove Scripture from its rightful place as the sole arbiter for God's will for believers. Scripture serves as a faithful guide as we navigate the varied voices that claim to speak for God. God's Word is indeed a light and lamp to our path as we attempt to live lives pleasing to our Maker.

Learning from the Past

Five hundred years ago Protestant Reformers like Martin Luther and those who later walked in their path like Francis Turretin took a life-threatening stand. Today, Christians must take an equally perilous position.

The disciples of Jesus have always been subject to persecution (John 15:18, 20). This can come from outside the church, be it from false religions or secular authorities bent on squashing Christian ideals. However, it can come from inside the church, too, from people who elevate personal experience to a position of higher authority than Scripture, to those who have such a low view of God's Word that when Christians say we must follow it, they scoff and show nothing but contempt.

Sola Scriptura, by Scripture alone. It is here that Protestants half a millennium ago made their stand against any supposed avenues of authority that were equal to God's Word, and it is here that Christians today must behave similarly.

> " In all cases, the Church is to be judged by the Scripture, not the Scripture by the Church. "
>
> **JOHN WESLEY (1703-1791)**[4]

BY SCRIPTURE ALONE

The law of the LORD
is perfect,
reviving the soul;
the testimony of the LORD
is sure,
making wise the simple;
the precepts of the LORD
are right,
rejoicing the heart;
the commandment of the LORD
is pure,
enlightening the eyes;
the fear of the LORD
is clean,
enduring forever;
the rules of the LORD
are true,
and righteous altogether.

Psalm 19:7-9

> **Your word** is a lamp to my feet and a light to my path.

Psalm 119:105

> You are my hiding place and my shield; I hope in **your word**.

Psalm 119:114

> All flesh is like grass and all its glory like the flower of grass. The grass withers, and the flower falls, but **the word of the Lord** remains forever.

1 Peter 1:24-25

> For as the rain and the snow come down from heaven
> and do not return there but water the earth,
> making it bring forth and sprout,
> giving seed to the sower and bread to the eater,
> so shall **my word** be that goes out from my mouth;
> it shall not return to me empty,
> but it shall accomplish that which I purpose,
> and shall succeed in the thing for which I sent it.

Isaiah 55:10-11

> Is not **my word** like fire, declares the LORD,
> and like a hammer that breaks the rock in pieces?

Jeremiah 23:29

> It is written, 'Man shall not live by bread alone,
> but **by every word** that comes
> from the mouth of God.'

Matthew 4:4

> By **grace** (that is to say, by favor) we are plucked out of Adam, the ground of all evil, and grafted into Christ, the root of all goodness. In Christ God loved us, his elect and chosen, before the world began, and reserved us unto the knowledge of his Son and of his holy gospel; and, when the gospel is preached to us, opens our hearts, and gives us **grace** to believe, and puts the Spirit of Christ in us; and we know him as our Father most merciful, and consent to the law, and love it inwardly in our heart, and desire to fulfil it … The blood of Christ obtained all things for us from God.[5]
>
> **WILLIAM TYNDALE**

Gratia
by Grace Alone

William Tyndale

1494 -1536 can be called the first prominent English-language Protestant. Fluent in at least seven languages, he broke then-existing laws by translating much of the Bible into English, which enraged government and church authorities. (At this time "official" Bibles in the church were in Latin, which most people who attended church could neither read nor understand.) Much of the famed King James Bible (completed in 1611) uses Tyndale's expressions and turns of phrase. He learned Greek and Hebrew for the sake of his translation work. His passion was for "the knowledge of [God's] Son and of his holy gospel" to be accessible to English Bible readers in their own native tongue. At the heart of Tyndale's insight into this gospel (good news) was his understanding of a New Testament word he translated as "grace". Tyndale's stance for grace was costly: he was eventually arrested, strangled, and burnt at the stake.

By Grace Alone

*For by grace you have been saved through faith.
And this is not your own doing; it is the gift of God,
not a result of works, so that no one may boast.
For we are his workmanship, created in Christ Jesus
for good works, which God prepared beforehand,
that we should walk in them.*
Ephesians 2:8-10

hree things are clear from the Bible passage above. First, people who have been "saved through faith" are God's "workmanship." Like a potter or toolmaker, God crafts His people "in Christ Jesus for good works." People who profess faith in Christ should be rich in actions and deeds that express their faith.

> Grace is explained as "not your own doing." It is also called "the gift of God, not a result of works."

Second, it is "through faith" that people are "saved." Faith is the means, or the avenue, by which they access the benefits of God's forgiveness, acceptance, and empowerment. This is explained in the next chapter of this book.

Third, and for this chapter most important, it is "by grace" that people "have been saved." Faith is the means, but at a more basic level, grace is the cause.

In the Scripture passage above this "grace" is explained as "not your own doing." It is also called "the gift of God, not a result of works." This presents a logical challenge. How can we be "created … for good works," and called on to exercise faith, yet at the same time be told that being saved is "not your own doing"? Does being "saved" mean believing and doing good works, or does it not?

Grace Generates Good Works

As far as William Tyndale was concerned, the answer to that question is easy. He wrote:

> For God gives no man His grace, that he should let it lie still and do no good as a result; but that he should increase it, and multiply it, and show it to others, and openly declare it, so that outward works provoke and draw others to God. As Christ says, "Let your light shine before others, so that they may see your good works and give glory to your Father who is in heaven" (Matt. 5:16). Otherwise, it would be like treasure buried in the ground, and concealed wisdom, in which there is no profit.[6]

Many passages in Scripture support this view. The Ephesians passage indicates that being saved "by grace through faith" leads naturally to "good works." The early Christian martyr Stephen, as a result of being "full of grace and power, was doing great wonders and signs among the people" (Acts 6:8; see also 14:3). Grace did not make him passive, idle, or complacent. It rather energized and equipped him.

Paul wrote, "But by the grace of God I am what I am, and his grace toward me was not in vain. On the contrary, I worked harder than any of them, though it was not I, but the grace of God that is with me" (1 Cor. 15:10). As a result of the grace Paul received, he "worked harder" than the other apostles. True, he gives full credit to "the grace of God that is with me." But that did not rule out—it rather supported and we may even say caused—the outpouring of effort he describes.

Paul uses the Greek word translated "grace" *(charis)* a hundred times in his New Testament writings. It has been pointed out that in his thirty years or so of ministry, he is known to have covered some 15,000 miles either on foot or on cramped and dangerous wooden boats.[7] He endured all this to spread the message of God's grace in Christ. This doesn't sound like someone who believed that grace means God does everything and people do nothing!

> Grace does not imperil or minimize the importance of good works but is rather the source.

Many other passages link grace with good works—in that order. Here is another example: "God is able to make all grace abound to you, so that having all sufficiency in all things at all times, you may abound in every good work" (2 Cor. 9:8). Grace does not imperil or minimize the importance of good works but is rather the source and origin of the good works that believers in Christ perform.

What Is Grace?

To cite William Tyndale again, he describes grace using the word "favor": "By grace I understand the favor of God, and also the gifts and working of his Spirit in us; as love, kindness, patience, obedience, mercifulness, despising worldly things, peace, concord, and such like."[8]

We all know what a favor is. We ask someone, "Would you do me a favor?" Perhaps we're flying somewhere with a friend, but our seat assignments are separate. We might ask another passenger to trade seats so we may sit together. If the other passenger says yes, it will not be because of payment or because we have authority to order the move. It will be by that other passenger's voluntary kindness. That's a picture of grace.

The New Testament also uses the helpful image of a gift: those

> "By grace I understand the favor of God, and also the gifts and working of his Spirit in us."
>
> **WILLIAM TYNDALE**

who believe in Christ "are justified by his grace as a gift" (Rom. 3:24). They receive a right standing before God not by making payment of some kind but rather as the result of God's free bestowal, his "gift."

Gift terminology also turns up when Paul contrasts Adam's sin with Jesus' saving death: "For if many died through one man's trespass, much more have the grace of God and the free gift by the grace of that one man Jesus Christ abounded for many" (Rom. 5:15). The outcome of this is bracing and glorious: "Those who receive the abundance of grace and the free gift of righteousness reign in life through the one man Jesus Christ" (Rom. 5:17). By "reign in life" Paul means enjoy the fruit of God's forgiveness, affirmation, guidance, and protection in this age, along with the promise of eternity in his presence in the age to come. What greater gift could be imagined?

Grace Has Long Been a Key Element in Christian Teaching

It is important to note that the grace-centered nature of the Christian message is not a new discovery. It was not even a new find of leaders like Tyndale, Luther, and Calvin at the Reformation. Rather, a long line of pastoral and theological leaders stretching back to the first century affirms that God saves the lost "by grace," that is, simply as an unmerited favor or a gift.

An important survey of church history finds the understanding of grace displayed in William Tyndale and in biblical writings present already, in various forms and to varying degrees, in the church fathers (AD 100-500), among medieval spiritual leaders (AD 500-1500), and in the writings of the pre-Reformers and the Reformers themselves (roughly AD 1500 and beyond).⁹

A few examples from the period of the church fathers will illustrate. Polycarp, a disciple of the apostle John, wrote to the Philippian congregation in the early second century, "Though you have not seen him, you believe in him with an inexpressible and glorious joy (which many desire to experience), knowing that by grace you have been saved, not because of works, but by the will of God through Jesus Christ."¹⁰ The first part of that verse draws on 1 Peter 1:8. The second part makes use of Ephesians 2:5, 8-9. Polycarp's understanding of grace underscores that it is not because of works that believers are saved. It is not even because of faith. Rather, it is "by grace," which he explains as "by the will of God through Jesus Christ."

Even before Polycarp, Clement of Rome (ca. AD 95) refers to grace repeatedly in his epistle to the Corinthians. Clement links Christ's saving death with the gift of repentance that makes saving faith in Jesus possible: "Let us fix our eyes on the blood of Christ and understand how precious it is to His Father, because, being poured out for our salvation, it

> "By grace you have been saved, not because of works, but by the will of God through Jesus Christ."

won for the whole world the grace of repentance." He calls the biblical writers "ministers of the grace of God." Grace is what makes the church and holds it together: "Do we not have one God and one Christ and one Spirit of grace that was poured out upon us?" In the history of God's people, His grace has strengthened not only apostles and prophets but women of faith too: "Many women, being strengthened by the grace of God, have performed many manly deeds."[11]

Grace Is Always an Issue—Grace *Alone*

It is widely recognized that at the Reformation, Roman Catholic teaching viewed grace as partially the result of human merit. Catholic scholar Erasmus clashed with Luther over this very point, resulting in Luther's famous tome *The Bondage of the Will*. Luther argued that since humans are lost in sin, it takes a work of grace to enable them to hear the gospel and place their faith in Jesus Christ. Grace precedes their act of faith. Without grace they could never exercise sufficient will to repent and be saved. Grace *alone* saves them; they can take no part of the credit. As Ephesians 2:9 puts it: "not a result of works, so that no one may boast."

> Grace *alone* saves them; they can take no part of the credit.

Erasmus' view, and the view of many still today, is that faith precedes grace. We believe in the gospel message, and as a result God bestows the gift of eternal life. However, this describes how we *experience* coming to faith. We hear, respond, and are saved. But it is too shallow an analysis of what went on behind the scenes to make our hearing and believing possible. Also, it risks making the act of believing into a meritorious deed—a "good work"—that saves us.

The two movements that work human salvation are captured wonderfully in John's Gospel: "But to all who did receive him, who believed in his name, he gave the right to become children of God, who were born, not of blood nor of the will of the flesh nor of the will of man, but of God" (John 1:12-13).

In a first movement, some "receive him" and "believed in his name." They became "children of God." But in a second (and prior) movement, there was a deeper will than the merely human will behind that faith decision: believers are "born, not of blood nor of the will of the flesh nor of the will of man, but of God."

A recent liberal writer, Michael Langford, underscores that salvation is not by grace alone, nor faith alone (see next chapter). He holds that today liberals side with Catholics in the view that "we can, to a degree, merit grace through good deeds."[12] This is in opposition to "the insistence of Luther and Calvin that 'all our righteousness is as filthy rags' (quoting Isa. 64:6), so that our salvation depends entirely on the unmerited gift of God."[13]

This same writer concedes that "there remains a tension with some conservative Protestants, who are not prepared to grant any significant role to human endeavor."[14] The tension here is actually not with "conservative Protestants" but with various Scripture verses that draw a sharp line between "grace" as a gift that humans have a hand in earning (the classic Catholic and Langford's liberal views), and "grace" as a mysterious gift of God's will apart from any human merit whatsoever.

Contrary to Langford's claim, Scripture *does* grant a "significant role to human endeavor." We showed that previously in the section that argues that grace does not rule out but assumes and generates good works. But this is as an expression of faith that, like grace itself, rests on God's promise, His will, and His work that precede our hearing and response. The gift of salvation "depends on faith, in order that the promise may rest on grace" (Rom. 4:16). God "saved us and called us to a holy

> The gift of salvation "depends on faith, in order that the promise may rest on grace".

calling, not because of our works but because of his own purpose and grace, which he gave us in Christ Jesus before the ages began" (2 Tim. 1:9). Can any human claim to have exercised faith "before the ages began"? Hardly. Therefore, it is by grace alone.

Practical Implications of *Sola Gratia*

We must be aware of certain issues related to *sola gratia*.

1. **"Grace alone"** can be twisted to imply "accept the gift of grace ... then go ahead and live like the devil if you want!" This is a misunderstanding and abuse of Scripture's teaching. Jude was written to early believers who encountered (in their churches!) "ungodly people, who pervert the grace of our God into sensuality and deny our only Master and Lord, Jesus Christ" (Jude 4). This may be compared to Paul's incredulous question and adamant reply: "What then? Are we to sin because we are not under law but under grace? By no means!" (Rom. 6:15).

Grace is not a license to sin but our entree to a life of faith in which believers "grow in the grace and knowledge of our Lord and Savior Jesus Christ" (2 Pet. 3:18). In this life we are, sadly, never free from sin (Rom. 3:23; 1 John 1:8, 10). But by grace we do progress in the direction of God's goodness, holiness, and love.[15]

> Grace is not a license to sin but our entree to a life of faith.

2 "Grace alone" is not just a slogan from the Reformation. It is a living truth that signals our release from crippling reliance on our goodness, achievement, or piety to make us "right with God." We may be able to convince ourselves for a time that we have made the right choices, pushed the right buttons, and taken the right steps to do what God demands to meet His standards. But the nagging voice returns: "Shouldn't you do even more?" And what about sins we commit after we've convinced ourselves that our deeds merit God's reward?

The quest to justify ourselves is a fool's errand, for it defies the repeated scriptural testimony that salvation is by grace. "But if it is by grace, it is no longer on the basis of works; otherwise grace would no longer be grace" (Rom. 11:6).

3 "Grace alone" provides us with a simple and clear way to glorify God. Scripture is clear: "Whatever you do, do all to the glory of God" (1 Cor. 10:31). But just how do we accomplish that? Another Scripture explains, and grace is at the center: God's saving work "is all for your sake, so that as grace extends to more and more people it may increase thanksgiving, to the glory of God" (2 Cor. 4:15).

As God's grace through the message of Christ goes forth, "more and more people" are thankful. God receives the praise he deserves. Those who praise him—we!—are deepened in fellowship with him and one another. This can occur by no other means than the mysterious and glorious working of God's grace.

4 "Grace alone" can apply the benefits of Christ's saving death and resurrection in AD 30 to our life situation in the twenty-first century. At the end of the William Tyndale quote at the beginning of this chapter we read, "The blood of Christ obtained all things for us from God." "Grace" is not an abstract principle but God's means of conveying the power of Jesus' work long ago to us in the present moment.

Scripture explains: "For you know the grace of our Lord Jesus Christ, that though he was rich, yet for your sake he became poor, so that you by his poverty might become rich" (2 Cor. 8:9). Here, what Jesus did to save us is called "the grace of our Lord Jesus Christ." He was rich with the Father in heaven in eternity past. But He took on human life—"he became poor"—so that we "by his poverty" can enjoy His gift of grace.

Sola gratia, by grace alone. William Tyndale suffered martyrdom for this and related convictions. Martin Luther's famous hymn contains these apt words, "The body they may kill: God's truth abideth still."

> "Let us then with confidence draw near to the throne of grace, that we may receive mercy and find grace to help in time of need."
> **HEBREWS 4:16**

BY GRACE ALONE

"But by **the grace of God** I am what I am, and **his grace** toward me was not in vain. On the contrary, I worked harder than any of them, though it was not I, but **the grace of God** that is with me."

1 Corinthians 15:10

"God is able to make all **grace** abound to you, so that having all sufficiency in all things at all times, you may abound in every good work."

2 Corinthians 9:8

> "But the free gift is not like the trespass. For if many died through one man's trespass, much more have **the grace of God** and the free gift by **the grace** of that one man Jesus Christ abounded for many."

Romans 5:15

> "For if, because of one man's trespass, death reigned through that one man, much more will those who receive the **abundance of grace** and the free gift of righteousness reign in life through the one man Jesus Christ."

Romans 5:17

> "For **by grace** you have been saved through faith. And this is not your doing; it is the gift of God, not a result of works, so that no one may boast."

Ephesians 2:8-9

> ... who saved us and called us to a holy calling, not because of our works but because of his own purpose and **grace**, which he gave us in Christ Jesus before the ages began.

2 Timothy 1:9

> But if it is **by grace**, it is no longer on the basis of works; otherwise **grace** would no longer be **grace**.

Romans 11:6

"What then? Are we to sin because we are not under law but under **grace**? By no means!"

Romans 6:15

"For you know **the grace** of our Lord Jesus Christ, that though he was rich, yet for your sake he became poor, so that you by his poverty might become rich."

2 Corinthians 8:9

3 Sola

> "This one and firm rock, which we call the doctrine of justification, ... is the chief article of the whole Christian doctrine, which comprehends the understanding of all godliness."[16]
> **MARTIN LUTHER**

Fide
through Faith Alone

Martin Luther

1483-1546 is rightly considered the father of the Protestant Reformation. Quick witted and quick tempered, Luther became a firebrand for biblical teaching, but only after he grew disillusioned as a Catholic monk and priest in the Augustinian monastic order. Luther astutely intuited that if Roman Catholic teaching was correct, and God could be appeased by good works, then God's righteousness was in question. As that was an impossibility, the only other option was that Catholic teaching was in error. His defiant stand against Pope Leo X and Emperor Charles V at the Diet of Worms in 1521, where Luther refused to recant of his "heresy," sealed his fate. Luther remained for the rest of his life an outlaw and heretic according to ecclesiastical and magisterial authorities. A Christian priest, monk, pastor, composer of hymns, author of catechisms, Bible translator, and theologian, Luther influenced German society, and ultimately all of Europe, like none before him. October 2017 marks the 500th anniversary of Luther's initial protest against Catholic teaching (his "95 Theses"). Half a millennium later, Christendom still experiences the effects of his reforming zeal.

Through Faith Alone

For we hold that one is justified by faith apart from works of the law.
ROMANS 3:28

ow can a sinner stand before a righteous and holy God? Much of the Protestant debate against Medieval Roman Catholicism centered on this important question. As we consider the biblical answer that the Protestants contended for, it would be helpful to bring the debate to modern times too. I can think of several ways that this question would be answered today.

- "There is no such thing as God, so the question is moot." If you believe the latest polls, somewhere around 13% of people in the western world consider themselves atheists, agnostics, or a-religious. That is by no means an insignificant number. Of course, by eliminating a righteous God, atheists have eradicated any real, objective measure of right and wrong. All that is left is a subjective, man-based morality that is either left to individuals or individual societies to establish, often with rather conflicting "norms."

- "The question is irrelevant." Every era has a generation of people who tend toward this answer. God is inconsequential to a large segment of our society. The Church consistently wrestles with ways to make Christianity "relevant" to these people. I say simply preach the Gospel and quote Jesus liberally. Jesus alone has the words of life (John 6:68) that are relevant to every soul.

- "God doesn't care." Since the Enlightenment, a large segment of western civilization has taken what is traditionally known as the "Deist" point of view. God is remote and uninterested in his creation. He put physical laws in place and then left the system to run on its own. Live your life as you see fit; God is far off doing whatever a disinterested God does. However, the incarnation of Jesus puts the lie to this view. God is not distant; he became one of us to redeem us.

- "God is only interested in your sincere attempts to live a good life." Along this line could be the similar "Just do your best" answer. As long as you really try to live a decent life, God will approve. This relativistic perspective yields a wishy-washy God who is convenient for those not wanting a divine Being looking over their shoulders. But sincerity is only as good as the object in which it is placed. Many people are sincerely wrong. Sincerity devoid of truth is simply misplaced zeal.

All of these responses have fatal flaws in their reasoning. I have noted some already, but the key deficiency is that none of these was the perspective of Jesus Christ. As such, Christians must immediately reject them. This leaves us with a response that sincere believers can debate: "A sinner can stand before a righteous and holy God by performing good works." Because this formed the heart of the Reformation protest, the remainder of this chapter will deal with why the Reformers contradicted this Catholic response, and what this means for us today.

Luther's Inner Turmoil

Martin Luther knew God is holy. The Old Testament clearly portrays this fact; Jesus Christ taught it, as did the authors of the New Testament. This being the case, Luther understood that God possesses perfect righteousness, such that anything contrary to His will must be opposed. That includes sinners who defiantly stand against Him.

> Luther understood that God possesses **perfect righteousness**, such that anything contrary to **His will** must be opposed.

The Medieval Roman Catholic Church was right on one score. The only way a sinner could ever have eternal communion with God was if the sinner was made righteous like God. However, the way that Catholic doctrine proposed was that the sinner, through good deeds, could work his way up toward spiritual perfection. As God did his part through the sanctifying grace of the seven sacraments of the Catholic Church, the individual also cooperated with this growing righteousness.[17]

However, Luther was deeply troubled by such a system. For starters, how could a sinner ever confess—and thus access the sanctifying grace of penance[18]—every single sin he ever committed if he could not recall them all? And if those unconfessed sins were not covered by the sacrament of penance, Luther knew that he himself would pay for them in the fires of Purgatory. The thought horrified him.

Whereas the typical monk attended to daily penance for minutes at a time, Luther drove his superiors crazy, literally spending hours fixating on it. However, for Luther this was supremely reasonable. After all, a perfectly holy God was judging matters, and Luther was a rotten sinner.

Luther's tender conscience was not his only problem. He also knew that he lacked the right heart. To put it bluntly, such a system that put the sinner in an almost constant state of fear did not engender love for God. In fact, Luther knew that deep in his heart he resented, and perhaps even hated, God for creating a standard that he could never attain.

The salvation scheme of Medieval Roman Catholicism produced fear in Luther, but it could equally produce pride in those who thought themselves good enough to warrant God's approval. It also was essentially selfish, as any system is when based on an individual's good works. The deeds are done to save one's own skin, after all, not usually out of gratitude to God. For this reason, John Calvin taught that "everyone who would obtain the righteousness of Christ must renounce his own."[19]

> Everyone who would obtain the righteousness of Christ must renounce his own.
> **JOHN CALVIN**

Luther's theological breakthrough came over many years; it was not an instantaneous epiphany. In lecturing through Psalms, Romans, Galatians, and Hebrews, Luther came to realize that God's righteousness was freely given in the gospel. Beforehand, he assumed God's righteousness was something that only condemns the sinner. Now Luther understood that this righteousness was a gift given by God and expressed through faith in the completed atoning work of Christ on behalf of the believer, as clearly seen in Paul's description of the gospel:

> "The righteous shall live by faith."

> For I am not ashamed of the gospel, for it is the power of God for salvation to everyone who believes, to the Jew first and also to the Greek. For in it the righteousness of God is revealed from faith for faith, as it is written, "The righteous shall live by faith." (Rom. 1:16-17)

Justifying Righteousness Freely Given by God, Not Earned by Humans

Both the English words "justification" and "righteousness" come from the same root word in Greek and are thus intimately related. Is a sinner made right (justified) in the eyes of God through his own good works, or through faith in the Good Work of Jesus on the cross? The Protestants rallied around the latter; justification is through faith alone, *sola fide*.

Catholicism taught that the righteousness that made the sinner justified before God came from inside the sinner, commonly referred to as "infused righteousness." However, the Reformers understood that people who by nature are spiritually dead in their trespasses (Eph. 2:1-3) can never attain the righteousness required to have a relationship with God. For Luther and others in the protest movement, justifying righteousness must be given to the sinner. It comes from outside him, thus it was known as "alien" or "imputed righteousness." It could never be earned by fallen creatures.

However, it *was* earned by Christ, through His perfectly sinless life. Luther spoke of the "great exchange" that took place between Christ and the sinner. As Jesus takes upon himself our sins (2 Cor. 5:21), he freely gives us his righteousness. Thus, the righteous requirements of God can be fully met in sinners (Rom. 8:4).

> For Luther and others in the protest movement, justifying righteousness must be given to the sinner.

This is why the Apostle Paul can write, "We know that a person is not justified by works of the law but through faith in Jesus Christ ... because by works of the law no one will be justified" (Gal. 2:16).

We must not forget that the Protestant Reformers were not creating some new theology or doctrine about salvation. Their intention was to "re-form" the church, to get it back to its original, biblical teaching. What Martin Luther was saying about *sola fide* had already been said by countless scholars and church fathers before him. For example, consider this statement by the apostolic father[20] Clement of Rome in one of his letters, commonly known as First Clement, penned near the end of the first century:

> And so we, having been called through His will in Christ Jesus, are not justified through ourselves or through our own wisdom or understanding or piety or works which we wrought in holiness of heart, but through faith, whereby the Almighty God justified all men that have been from the beginning; to whom be the glory for ever and ever. Amen.[21]

Another example is from the second-century Christian epistle, the Letter to Diognetus (9:5):

> O sweetest exchange! O unfathomable work of God! O blessings beyond all expectation! The sinfulness of many is hidden in the Righteous One, while the righteousness of the One justifies the many that are sinners.[22]

Of course, as evangelicals we should be more interested in what the Bible has to say about justification than what early church fathers said, yet it is encouraging just the same to see that these ecclesial forebears had a biblical perspective on justification that echoed that of the Reformers nearly a millennium and a half later.

For this reason, justification by faith has become a central tenet of varied Protestant denominations and bodies. For example,

- The Thirty-Nine Articles of the Church of England (Anglicanism) states in Article 11, "We are accounted righteous before God, only for the merit of our Lord and Savior Jesus Christ by faith, and not for our own works or deservings."[23]

- The Augsburg Confession of Lutheranism states in Article 4 that "men cannot be justified before God by their own strength, merits, or works, but are freely justified for Christ's sake, through faith, when they believe that they are received into favor, and that their sins are forgiven for Christ's sake, who, by His death, has made satisfaction for our sins. This faith God imputes for righteousness in His sight."[24]

- Reformed and Presbyterian churches have adopted the Westminster Confession of Faith, which says in chapter 11, "Those whom God effectually calls, He also freely justifies; not by infusing righteousness into them, but by pardoning their sins, and by accounting and accepting their persons as righteous; not for any thing wrought in them, or done by them, but for Christ's sake alone."[25]

- The First London Baptist Confession (1644) states in Article 28, "That those which have union with Christ, are justified from all their sins, past, present, and to come, by the blood of Christ; which justification we conceive to be a gracious and free acquittance of a guilty, sinful creature, from all sin by God, through the satisfaction that Christ hath made by his death; and this applied in the manifestation of it through faith."[26]

Practical Implications of *Sola Fide*

As we think about justification by faith alone, we must be careful to avoid the following errors:

1 First, we must not confuse justification with sanctification. Justification is a one-time "event" completed solely by God and is a determination about the state of the sinner apart from anything he might do. As such, a person cannot improve upon it or cooperate with it or add to it. The sinner's justification was determined before the foundation of the world (Eph. 1:4) and accomplished two thousand years ago at the crucifixion of Jesus. Because it is something that God determines, it cannot be lost or altered, and will eventually yield the glorification of the believer (Rom. 8:29-30).

Sanctification, on the other hand, is a process that the sinner cooperates in throughout his life as he is made into the image of God's Son. Justification eventually results in the sanctification and glorification of the believer. Protestants rightly saw that Roman Catholicism confused the two, as do many Christians today.

2 Second, we must not fashion faith as something the sinner does, such that it becomes a good work that is rewarded with eternal life. Faith is not something I muster up from within myself. It is a gift from God. As such, all boasting is excluded (Eph. 2:9).

3 Third, we must never think that faith merits something from God. As we saw in chapter 2, grace is unmerited favor from God. We are saved "by grace through faith" (Eph. 2:8).

4 Fourth, we must not think of faith as "blind" adherence to things we cannot otherwise prove. Christians do not take a "leap of faith." We trust God because he has made solid promises, he cannot lie, and he has proven himself trustworthy throughout his dealings with his children. This is why our faith must be biblically informed. Faith is only as good as the object in which it is placed. Our faith is placed in the living God who sent his Son Jesus into the world.

5 Fifth, we must not think of saving faith as inaction (similar to the previous chapter's discussion about grace and works). Biblical faith is belief in action. As the Reformers insisted, we are justified by faith alone, but not by a faith that is alone. In this way, the teaching of both Paul and James is reconciled. Paul is concerned with people who claim that they stand approved before God because of their good deeds. But Paul reminds them that works are the fruit of salvation, not the cause of it; works are a byproduct of salvation, not a prerequisite (Eph. 2:10).

To make his case, Paul points to Abraham, who was considered righteous because of his faith (Rom. 4:3-5).

However, James is concerned with people who claim to have faith in God yet have no godly works to show for it. In this case, James argues that living faith is verified by its fruit. "Faith apart from works is dead" (James 2:26). James also uses Abraham as an example of a man whose faith was proved by his works (2:21-23).

Perhaps one of the best biblical examples of how salvation does not come by one's good deeds, but simply on the basis of faith in Christ, is with the thief on the cross. Clearly this criminal had no opportunity to perform works that would merit his justification, and yet, Jesus promised him life in paradise (Luke 23:43). In what could be termed a "deathbed" conversion, the thief expressed saving faith in Jesus and was counted among the redeemed.

> One of the best biblical examples of how salvation does not come by one's good deeds, but simply on the basis of faith in Christ, is with the thief on the cross.

Incidentally, believers are not saved by faith, as if faith were a thing that can save a person. Rather, we are saved *through* faith (Eph. 2:8-9). Faith is the instrument through which Christ's saving work is imparted to the believer. And as the Reformers taught that even faith itself was a gift from God, this means that a sinner's justification comes solely as a free, unmerited gift, through the kindness and mercy of a loving heavenly Father.

Sola fide, by faith alone. The Protestant Reformers fought for this most precious doctrine, that the ungodly are freely justified through faith in the complete, perfect, atoning righteousness of Jesus Christ. Evangelicals must similarly affirm this belief today.

> Thus we simply interpret justification as the acceptance with which God receives us into his favor as if we were righteous; and we say that this justification consists in the forgiveness of sins and the imputation of the righteousness of Christ.[27]
> **JOHN CALVIN**

BY FAITH ALONE

> Yet we know that a person is not justified by works of the law but through **faith** in Jesus Christ, so we also have believed in Christ Jesus, in order to be justified by **faith** in Christ and not by works of the law.

Galatians 2:16

> For our sake he made him to be sin who knew no sin, so that in him we might become the righteousness of God.

2 Corinthians 5:21

" For by grace you have been saved through **faith**. And this is not your own doing; it is the gift of God, not a result of works, so that no one may boast. "

Ephesians 2:8-9

" As the body apart from the spirit is dead, so also **faith** apart from works is dead. "

James 2:26

"In Christ Jesus you are all sons of God, through **faith**."

Galatians 3:26

"Let us draw near with a true heart in full assurance of **faith**, with our hearts sprinkled clean from an evil conscience and our bodies washed with pure water."

Hebrews 10:22

> "This was according to the eternal purpose that he has realized in Christ Jesus our Lord, in whom we have boldness and access with confidence through our **faith** in him."

Ephesians 3:12

> "Without **faith** it is impossible to please him, for whoever would draw near to God must believe that he exists and that he rewards those who seek him."

Hebrews 11:6

Solus 4

> All that we have hitherto said of Christ leads to this one result, that condemned, dead, and lost in ourselves, we must in him seek righteousness, deliverance, life and salvation, as we are taught by the celebrated words of Peter, 'Neither is there salvation in any other: for there is none other name under heaven given among men whereby we must be saved.'[28]
>
> **JOHN CALVIN**

Christus
in Christ Alone

John Calvin

1509-1564 was born in France but eventually fled his Catholic homeland when he converted to Protestantism. Possessing a keen legal and theological mind, along with administrative and pastoral skills, Calvin settled in Geneva where he spent most of his life working to reform the church and magistrate there. His influence became international, helping to shape Christian communities in Scotland, Holland, Switzerland, England, France, and North America among others, and eventually even as far afield as South Africa and Korea. He penned what is arguably the most influential document of the Reformation, *The Institutes of the Christian Religion*. With it Calvin established himself as the premier theologian of his day, but he should also be remembered as a man of prayer who possessed the heart of a pastor.

In Christ Alone

*This is the testimony, that God gave
us eternal life, and this life is in his Son.
Whoever has the Son has life; whoever does
not have the Son of God does not have life.*
1 JOHN 5:11-12

Some time ago, I had a conversation with three mothers while we waited for our children who were attending an afternoon activity. The conversation quickly drifted to religion, and the three ladies each held the following perspectives. Lady 1 stated that whatever individuals believe is valid as long as they are sincere about it, it makes them better people, and it does no harm to others. Lady 2 believed in "G-O-D," the "great ordering deity," but she said we cannot know much at all about this deity, other than it exists. So live your life the best you can. Lady 3 was adamantly opposed to Christianity and especially the kind I was espousing, that there is only one way to have a relationship with God, through Jesus Christ. She had personally been taken up by an Indian guru who had been able to tell her incredible details about her life, things he could not have naturally known.

> There we stood, four of us, each with a different perspective on religious truth.

There we stood, four of us, each with a different perspective on religious truth. Granted, each woman had nothing but respect for the other ladies, and all of them were certain that my "only one way" position was in error.

Moving back in time, some two thousand years, the first-century world wasn't much different than that afternoon I spent with the three mothers.

Upon the first advent of Jesus, the Roman world had a multitude of gods and faiths and competing ethical systems. It was in this smorgasbord of religions that Jesus was born. After Christ's resurrection, his followers began to teach the exclusive truth that all other religions are false, and that the only way to have a relationship with the one, true God is through his Son. It was clearly a minority view in the opening decades of the first century.

Today, while perhaps not the minority view in some corners of the globe, the message of salvation only in Christ, *solus Christus*, is certainly an unpopular one in the western world. And let's not forget the 1.7 billion or so Muslims who believe that their way is the only way.

> The only way to have a relationship with the one, true God is through his Son.

In this chapter we will unpack some of the exclusive claims to salvation that Jesus and His disciples made two thousand years ago, and why those claims are still important today. However, before doing that, we need to set the stage for how *solus Christus* played a part in the Protestant Reformation.

Solus Christus
in Christ Alone

Who Mediates Between Sinners and God?

Both sides of the Protestant-Catholic debate during the Reformation agreed on one truth: sinners could not approach a holy and righteous God without a mediator. The Catholic answer to this dilemma posited that the clergy served that purpose, especially the priest who mediated the seven sacraments of the Catholic Church; he alone had the authority to stand between the sinner and God.

This system has a technical name for it: sacerdotalism. Perhaps you can see that this word has a similar root to words like sacred and sacrament. All of these have the basic understanding of making something holy. In a sacerdotal system, it is the priest who distributes the grace of the sacraments through which sinners can become holy. We spoke briefly about this in the *sola fide* chapter concerning the sacrament of penance. The priest intercedes for us by standing in the place of Christ and granting forgiveness of sins. Ultimately, as the "Vicar of Christ," the Pope stands at the top of this sacerdotal system, with the authority to grant forgiveness or withhold it.

> This system has a technical name for it: sacerdotalism. All of these have the basic understanding of making something holy.

Protestants objected to this system because it subtly removed Christ from his rightful place as our sole Mediator (1 Tim. 2:5). The book of Hebrews is an elaborate explanation of this priestly office of Christ. Jesus is a High Priest who has passed through the heavens (Heb. 4:14), is without sin (4:15), became "the source of eternal salvation" (5:9), established his priesthood on the basis of "the power of an indestructible life" (7:16), and who eternally makes intercession for those he saves (7:25). Chapter 8 of Hebrews explains that the new covenant under Jesus is superior to the old one under Moses, mainly because sacrifices are no longer to be offered over and over again. Jesus has offered the ultimate sacrifice "once for all" (7:27; 9:12, 26).

> Therefore he is the mediator of a new covenant, so that those who are called may receive the promised eternal inheritance, since a death has occurred that redeems them from the transgressions committed under the first covenant. (Heb. 9:15)

This once-for-all act of Jesus was dramatically portrayed in the Gospels when it is recorded that upon the crucifixion of Christ, the curtain in the temple was torn in two (Matt. 27:51; Mark 15:38; Luke 23:45). The curtain served to separate the Holy Place of the temple reserved for Jews, and the Most Holy Place reserved only for the High Priest. The author of Hebrews likens the curtain to Christ's body (Heb. 10:20). He writes about Jesus,

> He entered once for all into the holy places, not by means of the blood of goats and calves but by means of his own blood, thus securing an eternal redemption. (Heb. 9:12)

For these reasons, the Protestant Reformers could speak of the "priesthood of all believers." No longer do Christians need a go-between who intercedes between themselves and God. Jesus has done this, perfectly, completely, eternally. As such, each believer can approach God directly. "Let us then with confidence draw near to the throne of grace, that we may receive mercy and find grace to help in time of need" (Heb. 4:16). If we have sinned, we need not submit ourselves to an earthly priest who alone has the means by which we are forgiven. We can approach God directly, in the name and through the blood of Jesus. "If we confess our sins, he is faithful and just to forgive us our sins and to cleanse us from all unrighteousness" (1 John 1:9).

> No longer do Christians need a go-between who intercedes between themselves and God. Jesus has done this, perfectly, completely, eternally.

The Medieval Roman Catholic Church had dozens of mediators, similar to today. A Christian could ask for the Mother Mary to intercede, or one of the apostles, or any of the numerous saints who have died and gone directly to heaven. As already noted, the clergy also served as mediators. Contrary to all of these, the Reformers pointed to one and only one Mediator, Jesus Christ, who has now opened access for the believer to approach God directly.

The Problem of Exclusivity

While the debate for the Protestants was with the Roman Catholic belief that sinners stand justified before God through a combination of the atoning work of Christ and the sinner's own righteous acts, through the mediation of the priesthood, the debate for evangelical Christians today concerning *solus Christus* has more to do with competing claims from those who say they can intercede for people before our Maker.

Back to that conversation with the three mothers, the one problem they all had with my perspective was that they felt it was far too restrictive. They could not accept that relating to God was limited to just one way. Surely there are several, equally plausible means by which humans can connect with God?

I attempted to explain to them, though, that only one way makes reasonable sense. For starters, we all have the same problem. No matter our ethnicity or gender or geographic location or era in which we live, all humans have the same basic deficiency: we are sinners who stand condemned before a holy God. We need mediation. We need forgiveness. We need reconciliation.

Jesus made this very clear in His conversation with the Pharisee Nicodemus, when He told him that men are in darkness and suffer spiritual death. It is for this reason that they must be "born again" (John 3:3). We are all familiar with the "For God so loved the world" passage of John 3:16, but unfortunately the verses that follow are not so easily recalled. Here they are, and note as Jesus speaks what the problem is that all men and women face:

> For God did not send his Son into the world to condemn the world, but in order that the world might be saved through him. Whoever believes in him is not condemned, but whoever does not believe is condemned already, because he has not believed in the name of the only Son of God. And this is the judgment: the light has come into the world, and people loved the darkness rather than the light because their works were evil. (John 3:17-19)

Whenever I have pointed these verses out to people who are not familiar with them, their reaction is usually the same. They are surprised that immediately after John 3:16, which we all know is speaking about the love of God, that condemnation and judgment are the focus. However, this makes good sense once we understand what "salvation" is all about. Unfortunately, far too many Christians fashion "salvation" as being saved from financial or physical difficulties. For them, being saved means being promised a blessed life, a "healthy and wealthy" kind of living.

For Jewish followers at the time of Christ, "salvation" was at least initially understood as being rescued from Roman oppression. For this reason, even after the resurrection of Jesus, many of His disciples still expected the yoke of Roman tyranny to be lifted (e.g., Acts 1:6). Today, many people are quick to substitute their own ideas of salvation for the biblical message. In chapter 5, we will see some of these "gospels of human benefit."

In contrast to these false ideas about the mission of Jesus, we must embrace the hard truth that Jesus teaches about it. We have a problem and it is severe. We must be saved from none other than the wrath of a holy God. Later in that same John 3 passage we read the following words: "Whoever believes in the Son has eternal life; whoever does not obey the Son shall not see life, but the wrath of God remains on him" (3:36).

Note that God's wrath is on us as sinners, and unless we profess faith in Jesus, God's wrath "remains" on us. It is already there, and there is only one way to remove it. The one problem that plagues all of humanity requires the one solution to treat it. As fallen sinners, we need a heavenly righteousness. It is for this reason that both the Old and New Testaments consistently emphasize the need for atonement. It is why Jesus came into the world, to take upon Himself our sins, so that we could have a right relationship with God.

> Jesus came into the world, to take upon Himself our sins, so that we could have a right relationship with God.

In recording the words of the Apostle Paul, the New International Version of the Bible puts it this way:

> For all have sinned and fall short of the glory of God, and all are justified freely by his grace through the redemption that came by Christ Jesus. God presented Christ as a sacrifice of atonement, through the shedding of his blood—to be received by faith. (Rom. 3:23-25a)

"But there cannot possibly be only one way!" one of the mothers objected. But why not? In every other area of our lives, we know that there is truth and there is falsehood. Truth by its very nature excludes all "untruth." You cannot make a cake with sand instead of sugar simply because you sincerely believe you can. Despite how convenient it might be to your household budget, two plus two will never equal fifteen. Why in the area of religious truth do we expect things to be different? Why do so many people expect contradictory religious claims to all be right, just as long as you sincerely believe them?

Jesus said, "I am the way, and the truth, and the life. No one comes to the Father except through me" (John 14:6). Note the exclusive claims Jesus makes, and note the opposites of those claims. If you are not on the right way, then you are lost. If you do not know the truth, then you are wrong. If you do not have life, then you are dead.

There is only one solution to the universal problem of humanity. There is only one cure for what ails us all. God sent his Son into the world to save us from God's wrath and the punishment that we all rightly deserve because of our sin against him. Only then can we stand before God with a righteousness that is required, a righteousness freely given to us by Jesus. As John Calvin wrote with respect to *solus Christus*,

> To declare that we are deemed righteous, solely because the obedience of Christ is imputed to us as if it were our own, is just to place our righteousness in the obedience of Christ.[29]

While we concentrate on Christ when we speak about this *sola*, let us not forget that it is intimately related to the other *solas*. For example, if we rely on our own merit in order to stand before God, then our salvation is not in Christ alone. If I can somehow mediate for my own sins before God, then Jesus ceases to be the sole mediator.

The divine revelation of *solus Christus* is only known through *sola Scriptura*, and God's grace (*sola gratia*) and the gift of faith (*sola fide*) are given so that the believer might turn to Christ. Similarly, the Father is glorified (*soli Deo gloria*) by the work of his Son, a central focus of the earthly ministry of Jesus (John 17:1-5).

Practical Implications of *Solus Christus*

The practical implications of *solus Christus* are manifold.

1. First, we can have full confidence in Jesus and what he accomplished on our behalf through his perfect life and atoning death. We need not concern ourselves with our own works, wondering if we have done enough for God to justify us. Christ as our intercessory High Priest did all that was needed. The good deeds of believers can be done selflessly and out of gratitude for what God has done through Jesus.

2. Second, we must distrust any and all supposed mediators who claim to do what Jesus has already done. Any expectation that someone after Jesus is still needed, when the one and only Son of God has atoned for our sins, is pure deception.

3. Third, we can have full assurance that everything required to reconcile us to God has been accomplished in Jesus. Nothing more is needed. Who could possibly add to or complete what God's perfect Son has already accomplished "once for all?"

4. Fourth, an understanding of Christ as the only way should motivate Christians to faithfully witness this salvation to a fallen world. We must regain the sense of urgency that the original disciples had concerning the gospel. People who die apart from Jesus Christ are eternally

lost. No other way is available. If we who are saved do not share this message of hope, who will?

Solus Christus, in Christ alone. The fathers of the Reformation knew that only in Jesus could they have a right to stand before God. Christians today must similarly believe.

> "For there is one God,
> and there is one mediator
> between God and men,
> the man Christ Jesus,
> who gave himself as a ransom for all,
> which is the testimony given
> at the proper time."
>
> **1 TIMOTHY 2:5-6**

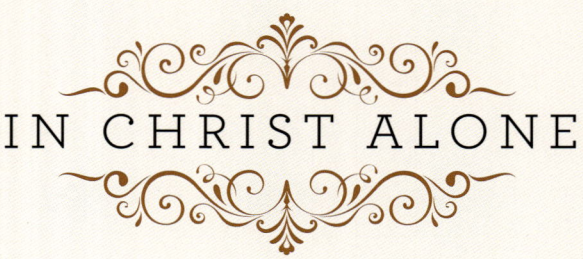

IN CHRIST ALONE

> If we confess our sins, he is faithful and just to forgive us our sins and to cleanse us from all unrighteousness.

1 John 1:9

> I am the way, and the truth, and the life. No one comes to the Father except through me.

John 14:6

> For I decided to know nothing among you except Jesus Christ and him crucified.

1 Corinthians 2:2

> Now to him who is able to do far more abundantly than all that we ask or think, according to the power at work within us, to him be glory in the church and in Christ Jesus throughout all generations, forever and ever.

Ephesians 3:20-21

> "There is neither Jew nor Greek,
> there is neither slave nor free,
> there is no male and female,
> for you are all one in **Christ** Jesus."
>
> ## Galatians 3:28

> "For we are his workmanship,
> created in **Christ** Jesus for good works,
> which God prepared beforehand,
> that we should walk in them."
>
> ## Ephesians 2:10

> So we, though many, are one body in **Christ**, and individually members one of another.

Romans 12:5

> There is therefore now no condemnation for those who are in **Christ** Jesus. For the law of the Spirit of life has set you free in **Christ** Jesus from the law of sin and death.

Romans 8:1-2

Soli Deo

5

> "The glory of God is, therefore, the chief and ultimate end for which man was created. It was for this purpose that God created rational and intelligent beings, such as angels and men, that knowing him, they might praise him forever. Hence, man was created principally for the glory of God; that is, for professing and calling upon his holy name, for praise and thanksgiving, for love and obedience, which consists in a proper discharge of the duties which we owe to God and our fellowmen. For the glory of God comprehends all these things.[30]"
>
> **ZACHARIAS URSINUS**

Gloria

for the Glory of God Alone

Zacharias Ursinus

1534-1583 was born in Germany. Gifted from childhood in areas like languages, philosophy, and theology, he was in contact with other Reformation leaders including Melanchthon, Bullinger, and Peter Martyr. He played a key role in the founding of the German Reformed Church, a group that favored Calvin's teachings in certain areas rather than Luther's. Ursinus was one of the major authors of the great statement of faith quoted below (p.106), the Heidelberg Catechism. He was remembered for his godliness, friendliness toward his students, and skill in defending key doctrines that came under attack during his brief era of ministry (he died at only 49).

For the Glory of God Alone

*"How can you believe, when you receive glory
from one another and do not seek
the glory that comes from the only God?"*
JOHN 5:44

Jesus' words quoted above indicate that people should seek God's glory. The place to start in this is believing in him. Zacharias Ursinus understood this, as the quote at the start of this chapter indicates. He sought to give God glory by composing a famous instructional manual called the Heidelberg Catechism (first published 1591). That catechism contains a total of 129 questions, but the first one, and its glorious answer, is the best known. Read it out loud slowly for maximum effect:

> **Q.** *What is your only comfort in life and in death?*[31]
>
> **A.** My only comfort in life and in death is that I am not my own, but belong—body and soul, in life and in death—to my faithful Savior, Jesus Christ.
>
> He has fully paid for all my sins with his precious blood, and has set me free from the tyranny of the devil. He also watches over me in such a way that not a hair can fall from my head without the will of my Father in heaven; in fact, all things must work together for my salvation.
>
> Because I belong to him, Christ by his Holy Spirit assures me of eternal life and makes me wholeheartedly willing and ready from now on to live for him.

To know Jesus through faith in him is to enjoy the infinite assurance of "comfort in life and in death," as the question puts it above. This makes possible the task that Jesus in John 5:44 expects of His listeners: seeking God's glory rather than merely human well-being and achievement.

This was an issue at the Reformation, and it has remained a pressing concern in churches and in Christian life ever since.

The Challenge of Seeking God's Glory Rather Than Our Own

It is well known that Martin Luther became disenchanted with the apparent worldliness and religious status-seeking of leaders in the Roman Catholic church as he knew it. When he visited Rome, he observed an opulence and gaudy greed that seemed to run counter to the Bible's stress on exalting God and him alone. He also came to realize that the cultic veneration of Jesus' mother Mary, of the saints, and of angels could not be justified from Scripture.

Scripture calls for exclusive worship of God,[32] and living foremost for God's glory alone. Venerating what is not God is idolatry. Sometimes even the institutional church can forget that. People professing to be Christians may lose their focus on God's glory and instead elevate their own holdings, achievement, and ambitions.

> Scripture calls for exclusive **worship of God,** and living foremost for **God's glory alone.**

While the principle *soli Deo gloria* ("for/to God alone be glory") was not articulated formally in the early years of the Reformation, it embodies a key concern of virtually all Reformation leaders. And not only of those leaders: it is also a key concern of Scripture itself. Two examples will illustrate, one from Old Testament times and another from the New.

In the time of Jeremiah (ca. 600 BC), God's people in Judah had turned away from the true God. As God asks accusingly, "Has a nation changed its gods, even though they are no gods? But my people have changed their glory for that which does not profit" (Jer. 2:11). Here "their glory" is God himself. By turning to other gods, Judah had abandoned God in his magnificence, perfection, and radiant splendor (all aspects of his "glory").

In this foreboding time, just before God's judgment of Judah in 587 BC, God asks one of his followers a key question: "And do you seek great things for yourself?" (Jer. 45:5). The implied answer is yes. God addressed the question to Jeremiah's scribe, Baruch. The tiny chapter of Jeremiah 45 pictures Baruch bemoaning his labor. He is weary and discouraged. Evidently he expected more blessing from God than he felt he was receiving for his faithful service under trying, even dangerous circumstances.

God sternly warns Baruch, "And do you seek great things for yourself? Seek them not" (Jer. 45:5). God's followers are on this earth to promote God's reputation and honor and recognition, not their own. True, God in his generosity may and often does reward those who seek him. But Baruch lost sight of the fact that we serve God first for his sake, not for what we can gain for ourselves.

> We serve **God first for his sake,** not for what we can gain for ourselves.

In effect, God reminded Baruch of what Christians pray regularly: "Thy kingdom come … For Thine is the kingdom, and the power, and the glory forever." God's glory, not self-benefit, is the highest aim of all who follow God in true faith. *Soli Deo gloria!*

In New Testament times, Paul made the famous statement to the Corinthians, "So, whether you eat or drink, or whatever you do, do all to the glory of God" (1 Cor. 10:31). Many in the Corinthian church were failing at this. They had split into factions. They were gripped by jealousy and strife (3:3). They sinned flagrantly and boasted about it (5:6). This infected the entire church. Paul feared that some did not even know God (15:34). Where had they gone wrong?

"Countless guides" (false teachers) had entered the picture at Corinth (4:15). They arrogantly (4:18) sought to adjust Paul's message of Christ crucified (1:23). It is easy to imagine why. A message of wealth and power (4:8) is more pleasant than one of self-sacrifice and service.

> God's glory, not self-benefit, is the highest aim of all who follow God in true faith.

Yet Jesus who died for sin calls his followers to take up their own cross and follow him. This was the example of the apostles (4:9-13). Paul urges the Corinthians to imitate Paul and the other apostles in this (4:16).

In other words, Paul's theology was a theology of the cross. The practical Christian life is one of seeking God's honor and glory, not our own benefit. As he tells the Corinthians later, God "has shone in our hearts to give the light of the knowledge of the glory of God in the face of Jesus Christ" (2 Cor. 4:6).

> The practical Christian life is one of seeking God's honor and glory, not our own benefit.

The Corinthians had turned the gospel message around so that it was about them, not about Christ. Instead of a theology of the cross which exalts God, they had slipped into a self-seeking outlook (like that of Baruch) that set them at odds with the Bible's truth in its deepest and broadest sense.

The knowledge of the glory of God...

The Good and the Best: Gospels of Human Benefit

Scripture warns of those who "loved the glory that comes from man more than the glory that comes from God" (John 12:43). Jesus himself did not "receive glory from people" (5:41) or seek his own glory (8:50). It is all the more lamentable, then, that in recent memory the good news of Christ has been intermingled, or even replaced, with a message of human self-promotion. This is not to say the church explicitly denies the importance of recognizing God in his unique heavenly radiance, his "immortal, invisible" grandeur (1 Tim. 1:17). Rather, the church may quietly drift into equating God with the benefits he promises and grants. Human benefit then becomes the highest goal and ideal even among those professing faith in Jesus.

Consider some gifts that God may well grant, but which are themselves not part of his offer of salvation and his call to faithful service in the gospel message of Christ—crucified, raised, ascended, and one day returning:

Health. Good health is a blessing from God (3 John 2). Prayers for sickness are mandated in Scripture (James 5:14). Jesus healed many of all kinds of ailments. Yet he did not heal everyone. Apostles like Paul also worked miracles of healing (Acts 19:11-12), but on other occasions Paul could not heal his own co-workers (1 Tim. 5:23; 2 Tim. 4:20). In modern times "faith healers" have made "Jesus" into a magic word claiming to cure medical ills. But what about sin and the sickness of the soul? Jesus said, "By this my Father is glorified, that you bear much fruit and so prove to be my disciples" (John 15:8). This fruit centers in the glory of obeying and spreading the gospel, not just in improving medical conditions, however wonderful physical healing may be when God grants it.

Wealth.

Certain Bible verses taken out of context can be used to promote the notion that the more (money) we give to a religious cause, the more (money) we will eventually amass. See, for example, Luke 6:38: "Give, and it will be given to you. Good measure, pressed down, shaken together, running over, will be put into your lap." Yet neither Jesus, nor the apostles, nor the early church in Acts, connect saving faith in Christ with monetary plenty. In fact, there are repeated warnings against riches and their misuse.[33] Since God may grant material prosperity, it is understandable that we seek it from him through prayer and our life's labor. But "riches do not last forever; and does a crown endure to all generations?" (Prov. 27:24). The answer to this question is no! The chief glory God bestows is forgiveness and a relationship with him, things that *do* last forever. The glory of earthly wealth is fleeting. It is tragic that today ministries around the world fund jets and mansions for preachers. Financial empires are built on the backs of offerings of poor people who believe preachers' lies that by giving (to the preachers!) they will get more money for themselves.

Security.

The Bible offers promise of "abundance of prosperity and security" (Jer. 33:6). "Jerusalem shall dwell in security" (Zech. 14:11) in the end time. We all want lives that are safe and surroundings that are secure. But as Nigerian Christians have found in the era of Boko Haram, faithful believers are not always spared the fury of gospel enemies. Old Testament prophets were often punished for their witness. The early church wrestled with the problem of suffering for their faith in Jesus: "As it is written, 'For your sake we are being killed all the day long; we are regarded as sheep to be slaughtered'" (Rom. 8:36, quoting Ps. 44:22). God is glorified when people dwell in peace. But he is also glorified when his followers suffer for his name's sake. Many modern-day martyrs have rightly chosen eternal security through remaining faithful unto death. God will avenge their blood to his glory (Rev. 12:11). Those who choose earthly security over faithfulness gain short-term advantage but lose out on the benefit of glorifying God.

Other human ideals could be cited: *Freedom. The status of recognition by others. "Happiness" in the sense of what those around us treasure and enjoy.* None of these is necessarily evil in itself. "Every good gift and every perfect gift is from above, coming down from the Father of lights" (James 1:17) On occasion Scripture speaks of the way God grants a certain glory to humans: "Yet you have made him a little lower than the heavenly beings and crowned him with glory and honor" (Ps. 8:5). God is not selfish or stingy with his infinite goodness and light!

But the question is, "What are people created for? Why does God grant the gift of eternal life to those who trust in Christ?" It is not so they can spend their lives seeking their own honor. Over 300 times the Bible uses the word "glory" with reference to God. The time is coming when "all the earth shall be filled with the glory of the Lord" (Num. 14:21). A key Reformation insight is that followers of Christ devote their lives to the enterprise of God's magnification, acclaim, and worship. When these come at the expense of believers' own temporal benefit, they are prepared to make the sacrifice. Their prayer is that of the psalmist: "Not to us, O Lord, not to us, but to your name give glory, for the sake of your steadfast love and your faithfulness!" (Ps. 115:1).

Practical Implications of *Soli Deo Gloria*

The priority of God's glory for all of life is more than an important theological principle reaffirmed at the Reformation. Numerous implications for everyday life follow, including the following seven:

1 *God's glory means his people live in eschatological readiness.*

Jesus said, "Whoever is ashamed of me and of my words, of him will the Son of Man be ashamed when he comes in his glory and the glory of the Father and of the holy angels" (Luke 9:26). We do not want the Son of Man to be ashamed of us at his return! So we devote our energies to pursuits that glorify God rather than simply please ourselves (Rom. 15:3).

2 *Suffering is often part of entering into Christ's glory.*

On the Emmaus Road Jesus reasoned, "Was it not necessary that the Christ should suffer these things and enter into his glory?" (Luke 24:26). Yes, it was. Therefore, since a servant is not greater than his master, followers of Jesus can expect rough times as God readies them for glory in the age to come. Scripture teaches this approach to interpreting hardships endured for the sake of pleasing the Lord: "Light momentary affliction is preparing for us an eternal weight of glory beyond all comparison" (2 Cor. 4:17). "If anyone suffers as a Christian, let him not be ashamed, but let him glorify God in that name" (1 Peter 4:16).

3 *The life of Jesus is a study in true earthly glory.*
In John's Gospel the author writes, "And the Word became flesh and dwelt among us, and we have seen his glory, glory as of the only Son from the Father, full of grace and truth" (John 1:14). Jesus was the most glorious human ever to walk the earth, but his life was filled with testing, sacrificial dedication growing out of fervent prayer, and reaching out to others. Do we yearn for the glories Jesus spoke of, promised, and exhibited? Drawing life lessons from the unassuming "glory" glimpsed in Jesus' life can provide valuable lessons for our own.

4 *To withhold glory from God is a grave offense.*
A high government official, Herod Agrippa I, reveled in the praise of people and opposed Jesus' followers (Acts 12:1). Because of his insolence, "Immediately an angel of the Lord struck him down, because he did not give God the glory, and he was eaten by worms and breathed his last" (Acts 12:23). This gruesome incident is a reminder of how seriously God takes his place of unique exaltation. It is wise for all of us to give attention to whether we are fully devoted to God's glory.

5 *We do not fully attain God's glory in this life.*

The apostle Paul exults in knowing Christ: "Through him we have also obtained access by faith into this grace in which we stand." But in the same verse he affirms, "We rejoice in hope of the glory of God" (Rom. 5:2). Here "hope" refers to what God will one day reveal rather than what believers at present realize or acquire. God's glory directs our present lives, but it also motivates us with the prospect of untold wonders in future times. We can endure present frustrations and hardships, because coming glories will have the last word. "When Christ who is your life appears, then you also will appear with him in glory" (Col. 3:4).

6 *Simple everyday acts bring glory to God.*

God's glory and glorifying God can seem like lofty matters out of the reach of everyday believers. But Paul, in urging Christians to be hospitable, states: "Therefore welcome one another as Christ has welcomed you, for the glory of God" (Rom. 15:7). Simple hospitality glorifies God. So does daily living in accordance with God's commands and expectations: "So glorify God in your body" (1 Cor. 6:20). It's not about advanced degrees, extensive formal training, or heroic acts. "Ordinary" believers can and should live daily lives in such a way "that in everything God may be glorified through Jesus Christ" (1 Pet. 4:11).

7 *God's glory is the source of Christian flourishing.*

God's glory is not a mysterious heavenly glow and aura that believers can only glimpse and fear. From that "glory," the radiance of God's good and perfect presence, flow everything believers need to live and serve him: "And my

God will supply every need of yours according to his riches in glory in Christ Jesus" (Phil. 4:19). We may think of God's glory as a warehouse stocked with all we need for realizing his will in our lives. We pray to and commune with a God whose "glory" is not remote and impersonal. It is rather near to those who seek God in ways that will enable him to show his glory through them.

No One Like God in His Glory

Banished to the island of Patmos, John the apostle posed a pressing question with a glorious answer: "Who will not fear, O Lord, and glorify your name? For you alone are holy" (Rev. 15:4). His answer in that same verse: "All nations will come and worship you, for your righteous acts have been revealed."

All who know God through faith in Christ rejoice at the privilege they enjoy. God has created us, claimed us as his children, and enables us to leave behind the deadly futility of self-seeking in this brief life. Instead, we can seek the sole glory of the sole true God revealed in his Son Jesus Christ.

Soli Deo Gloria!
For the Glory of God Alone.

> " For from him and through him
> and to him are all things.
> To him be glory forever. Amen. "
> **ROMANS 11:36**

FOR THE GLORY OF GOD ALONE

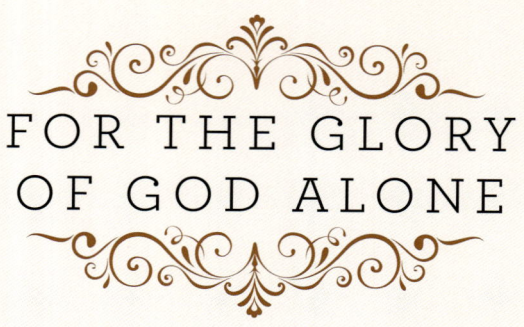

"So, whether you eat or drink, or whatever you do, do all to **the glory of God**."

1 Corinthians 10:31

"God, who said, "Let light shine out of darkness," has shone in our hearts to give the light of the knowledge of **the glory of God** in the face of Jesus Christ."

2 Corinthians 4:6

"To the King of the ages, immortal, invisible, the only God, be honor and **glory** forever and ever. Amen."

1 Timothy 1:17

"But truly, as I live, and as all the earth shall be filled with the **glory** of the Lord."

Numbers 14:21

> For this light momentary affliction is preparing for us an eternal weight of **glory** beyond all comparison.

2 Corinthians 4:17

> Not to us, O Lord, not to us,
> but to your name give **glory**,
> for the sake of your steadfast love
> and your faithfulness!

Psalm 115:1

> "Yet if anyone suffers as a Christian, let him not be ashamed, but let him **glorify** God in that name."
>
> ## 1 Peter 4:16

> "The Word became flesh and dwelt among us, and we have seen his **glory**, glory as of the only Son from the Father, full of grace and truth."
>
> ## John 1:14

A Final Word
Semper reformanda!

This book has explained the Reformation *solas*. It has been written to encourage their rediscovery today.

The Latin *semper reformanda* is often rendered "always reforming." Some take this to mean now is the time to reconceptualize God, Scripture, the church, and all they stand for. Nothing is really fixed; we can take it upon ourselves to create new truths for a new religion that gets rid of things in Scripture and church teaching that we in our times may not like.[1]

This has been the method of too much Western theology and preaching since around 1800. The result is clear in the thousands of empty churches across much of Europe, and the shrinking numbers in "liberal" denominations in the United States and elsewhere in the world where the Bible has been interpreted in ways that deny its own assertions.

Christian scholar Michael Horton points out that the phrase *semper reformanda* first appeared in 1674.[2] Its author was a Dutch Reformed pietist named Jodocus van Lodenstein. He used it to explain that "the lives and practices of God's people always need further reformation." God, Scripture, and established core doctrines do not change with the generations. It is people, including the church, that stray from the path of truth and need ongoing adjustment to stay in step with God's truth and leading.

Horton defines and interprets the phrase:

> "The church is reformed and always [in need of] being reformed according to the Word of God." The verb is passive: the church is not "always reforming," but is "always being reformed" by the Spirit of God through the Word. Although the Reformers themselves did not use this slogan, it certainly reflects what they were up to; that is, if one quotes the whole phrase!

Too much Western theology has turned away from the God presented in Scripture. Too many Western "Christians" do not know God! It is an old problem. An apostle had to say to a church he had founded, "Wake up from your drunken stupor, as is right, and do not go on sinning. For some have no knowledge of God. I say this to your shame" (1 Cor. 15:34).

At the same time, the Spirit of this "God, who through Christ reconciled us to himself" (2 Cor. 5:18), has been poured out in nations around the world in unprecedented numbers.

It has been pointed out that "theology is not just about arithmetic."[3] Numbers of converts do not necessarily demonstrate the truth of what multitudes affirm. But as professor Lamin Sanneh states, "Religion is not about deserted pews, either."[4] The authors of *In Christ Alone* believe that the global surge in confessing Christians lends support to the credibility of the *solas* that marked the Reformation and are being rediscovered worldwide today.

It is our prayer that the *solas* will resonate in readers and encourage them in the direction of the model follower of Christ, whom he described as "like a master of a house, who brings out of his treasure what is new and what is old" (Matt. 13:52).

Think of "new" as your life and setting. We come to God, the Ancient of Days, as a child of our times.

Think of "old" as God—Father, Son, and Holy Spirit. Think of Scripture. Think of the heritage of the faithful, some described in the chapters of this book.

Most of all, think of Christ. To be "in him," by grace through faith, is to find yourself "a new creation. Old things have passed away. Look! New things have arrived!" (2 Cor. 5:17, paraphrased).

In a rapidly changing world, our knowledge of God and relationship with him require continual upgrading and renewal. We repent, we worship, we serve in keeping with the "new things" God shows his people about his steadfastness and their need for him. *Semper reformanda!*

But while our life circumstances may morph with blurring speed, in Christ we find stability to steer us while God gives us breath.

> "Jesus Christ is the same yesterday and today and forever."
> **HEBREWS 13:8**

End Notes

Dedication

[1] Johnson, Zurlo, Hickman, and Crossing, "Christianity 2017," *International Bulletin of Missionary Research* 41/1 (January 2017) 41-52.

Preface

[1] Composed by Stuart Townend and Keith Getty.

[2] This is recounted by David Garrison in research for his book *A Wind in the House of Islam: How God is Drawing Muslims Around the World to Faith in Jesus Christ* (Monument, CO: WIGTake Resources, 2014). The citation above is from http://www.premierchristianity.com/Past-Issues/2016/June-2016/Muslims-turning-to-Christ-a-global phenomenon?utm_source=Premier+Christian+Media&utm_medium=email&utm_campaign=7174621_Christianity+03%2F06%2F16&utm_content=Muslims&dm_i=16DQ%2C49RZ1%2CKILLHS%2CFLXGD%2C1 . Accessed February 15, 2017.

[3] In John 1:1, He is called the Word, the *logos*. In 1:14 we read He took on flesh. "At the Father's side" (1:18) echoes "with God" (1:1).

[4] For a recent academically rigorous but theologically sensitive analysis of the solas see Kevin J. Vanhoozer, *Biblical Authority after Babel: Retrieving the* Solas *in the Spirit of Mere Protestant Christianity* (Grand Rapids: Brazos, 2016).

[5] Dale B. Martin, *Biblical Truths: The Meaning of Scripture in the Twenty-First Century* (New Haven and London: Yale University Press, 2017), 35.

[6] Ibid., 260.

[7] Ibid., 260-261.

[8] M. Craig Barnes, "The pastors I worry about," *Christian Century*, January 4, 2017, 35.

[9] Lamin Sanneh, *Whose Religion Is Christianity? The Gospel Beyond the West* (Grand Rapids, MI/Cambridge, UK: Eerdmans, 2003), 14.

[10] Rodney Stark and Xiuhua Wang, *A Star in the East: The Rise of Christianity in China* (West Conshohocken, PA: Templeton Press, 2015), 115.

[11] Downers Grove: InterVarsity, 2011, 228.

[12] For these figures see Todd M. Johnson, Gina A. Zurlo, Albert W. Hickman, and Peter Crossing, "Christianity 2017: Five Hundred Years of Protestant Christianity," *International Bulletin of Missionary Research* 41/1 (January 2017) 50.

[13] Open Doors. They limit their count to eyewitness accounts.

[14] Center for the Study of Global Christianity, Gordon-Conwell. See Mendy Belz, "Numbers matter," *World Magazine*, Feb. 18, 2017, p. 32. This study center includes all who have died as the result of being Christians, including those killed in war.15

[15] Johnson, Zurlo, Hickman, and Crossing, "Christianity 2017," *International Bulletin of Missionary Research* 41/1 (January 2017) 50.

[16] *Whose Religion Is Christianity?*, 70.

[17] For the account see http://chewelahindependent.com/man-dies-falling-tree-well-49-degrees-north/. Accessed February 15, 2017.

Chapters 1-5

[1] John W. Beardslee III (ed.), *The Doctrine of Scripture: Locus 2 of Institutio Theologiae Elencticae* (Grand Rapids: Baker, 1981) 39–40.

[2] John Calvin, Henry Beveridge (ed.), *Institutes of the Christian Religion* (Grand Rapids: Eerdmans, 2013) 1.6.3.

[3] Roland Bainton, *Here I Stand* (New York: Mentor, 1950) 90.

[4] *The Works of the Rev. John Wesley*, vol. 15 (London: Thomas Cordeux, 1812) 180.

[5] William Tyndale, *A Pathway into Holy Scripture*, in *Doctrinal Treatises and Introductions to Different Portions of the Holy Scriptures by William Tyndale, Martyr, 1536*, ed. Henry Walter (Cambridge: Cambridge University Press, 1848), 14-15. Some wording has been updated. Underlining added.

[6] Ibid., 60. Wording has been adapted and updated. The Matthew verse is from the ESV.

[7] Eckhard Schnabel, *Early Christian Mission* (Downers Grove: InterVarsity, 2004), 2:1288.

[8] Tyndale, *Obedience of a Christian Man*, in *Doctrinal Treatises*, 286.

[9] See the survey of these periods in Stephen J. Lawson, *Pillars of Grace AD 100-1564* (Lake Mary, FL: Reformation Trust, 2011), chapter 1.

[10] *The Apostolic Fathers*, trans. J. B. Lightfoot and J. R. Harmer, ed. and rev. by Michael W. Holmes, 2d ed. (Grand Rapids: Baker, 1989). The quote comes from Polycarp's *Letter to the Philippians* (Phili. 1:3).

[11] Ibid. Quotations come from 1 Clement 7:4; 8:1; 46:6; 55:5.

[12] Michael J. Langford, *The Tradition of Liberal Theology*, 2d ed. (Grand Rapids/Cambridge: Eerdmans, 2014), 50-51 (quote on 50).

[13] Ibid.

[14] Ibid., 51.

[15] For current abuses and misrepresentations of the Bible's teaching on grace, see the important book by Wayne Grudem, *Free Grace Theology: 5 Ways It Diminishes the Gospel* (Wheaton: Crossway, 2016).

[16] From Luther's 1538 commentary on Galatians, cited in Herbert Bouman, "The Doctrine of Justification in the Lutheran Confessions," *Concordia Theological Monthly*, Vol. XXVI, No. 11, November 1955.

[17] Believers who in this life attain this perfect level of righteousness are declared "saints" by the Catholic Church and immediately upon death enter into heaven. The vast majority of people go to Purgatory first, where their sins not covered by the atoning work of Christ as accessed through the sacraments are purged through suffering.

[18] The Catholic sacrament of penance is often wrongly called "confession," but confession is merely one step in the process of penance. Proper penance involves four steps: 1) feeling guilt, 2) confessing the sin, 3) receiving absolution from the priest, who stands in the place of Christ and can offer forgiveness, and 4) performing satisfaction, which is a good deed done by the sinner to produce positive righteousness.

[19] *Institutes*, 3.11.13.

[20] "Apostolic fathers" is a term used to designate those early church leaders who came immediately after the original apostles.

[21] 1 Clement 32:4, Early Christian Writings, www.earlychristianwritings.com/text/1clement-lightfoot.html, accessed December 30, 2016.

[22] Christian Classics Ethereal Library, www.ccel.org/ccel/richardson/fathers.x.i.ii.html, accessed December 31, 2016.

[23] Anglicans Online, http://anglicansonline.org/basics/thirty-nine_articles.html, accessed January 3, 2017.

[24] Book of Concord, http://bookofconcord.org/augsburgconfession.php, accessed January 3, 2017.

[25] Center for Reformed Theology and Apologetics, www.reformed.org/documents/wcf_with_proofs/, accessed January 3, 2017.

[26] The Reformed Reader, www.reformedreader.org/ccc/h.htm, accessed January 3, 2017.

[27] *Institutes*, 3.11.2

[28] *Institutes*, 2.16.1.

[29] *Institutes*, 3.11.23.

[30] Adapted from Zacharias Ursinus, *The Commenary of Dr. Zacharius Ursinus on the Heidelberg Catechism* (trans. G. W. Williard; Phillipsburg, NJ: Presbyterian and Reformed, n.d.), 28.

[31] Adopted with slight alteration from the version found at www.rca.org/heidelberg, accessed December 28, 2016.

[32] "No other gods": see Exod. 20:3; Deut. 5:7. "No other god": see Exod. 34:14; Isa. 45:21; Dan. 3:29. Jesus affirmed the same truth (Matt. 4:9; Luke 4:8).

[33] Prov. 11:4, 28; 28:20; Matt. 19:23; Luke 12:21; 1 Tim. 6:9; James 1:10-11

A Final Word

[1] This is the impression given in Dale Martin's *Biblical Truths: The Meaning of Scripture in the Twenty-First Century*. These "truths" are often the opposite of what Scripture teaches and what churches worldwide have historically confessed.

[2] See the posting "Semper Reformanda" at http://www.ligonier.org/learn/articles/semper-reformanda/. Accessed February 16, 2017. Citations in this paragraph and the next are from this posting.

[3] *Whose Religion Is Christianity?*, 57.

[4] Ibid.

Victor Kuligin (DTh, University of Stellenbosch) is a senior lecturer at Bible Institute of South Africa in the Cape Town suburbs, where he has also served as Academic Dean. Previously he spent fourteen years as a missionary in Namibia, where he lectured at Namibia Evangelical Theological Seminary. He is an author and international speaker, guest lecturing in countries like India, Bulgaria, Sudan, Ethiopia, and Rwanda.

Robert Yarbrough (PhD, University of Aberdeen) is professor of New Testament at Covenant Theological Seminary in St. Louis, Missouri, USA. He taught previously at Trinity Evangelical Divinity School and Wheaton College. He is author, co-author, or translator of numerous books and articles. He has been involved in theological education in Africa (Egypt, Sudan, South Sudan, South Africa) since 1989.